Vegetable Gardening in the Southern United States

Your Guide to Plan, Grow, Gather, and Preserve Year-Round

S. A. Glover

Table of Contents

Introduction

The glory of gardening: hands in the dirt, head in the sun, heart with nature. To nurture a garden is to feed not just on the body, but the soul. –Alfred Austin

Vegetable gardening, an occupation as old as time, has steadily become the norm in American society. In a world where any supermarket offers a huge variety of produce, more and more American families decide to establish vegetable gardens at home, not only as a hobby, but also as a way to lower everyday costs.

According to the National Gardening Association, one in every three families decide to grow their own produce at home. The reasons behind this statistic are several: economic need, gardening as a productive hobby, or just the fact that homegrown food tastes better.

Having a garden at home and producing your own vegetables has many benefits that go beyond the mere economic aspect. Homegrown produce is cleaner, cheaper and tastier than produce sold in big supermarkets. The effort and time you put into your garden will not only give you a palpable result, but it will influence your mood, your health, both mental and physical, and it can be a way to relate to others around you by sharing the garden activities and the harvested produce. You can even sell your surplus.

There are many reasons why people do not take the initial step into gardening at home. For example, in the hectic modern lifestyle people have less and less time to devote to their hobbies. Also, information about what gardening entails is not always clear, so a lot of people are under the impression that gardening is difficult and out of reach for the everyday person. It just might be that people living in smaller spaces do not have a place they deem fit to start gardening. Even people who have the backyard space and free time that could be devoted to gardening are hesitant to start, unsure of how to do it, what it entails, confused by the tidbits of information that they've heard and don't know how to combine it all in an organic way.

All these concerns are valid, but not impossible to overcome. As we will see from the start of this book, you can grow a garden almost anywhere, provided that certain requirements are met. It is all in the planning.

This is the intent of this book: to guide you through the planning, the growing and the harvesting of your own produce, according to your needs, and in a way that can be applied to every household, no matter the space or your abilities.

The focus of this book will be planting in the USDA Hardiness Zones 7, 8 and 9 that comprise most of the Southern United States, but the basic notions of gardening can be applied to any place you find yourself living in. Therefore, if you happen to come across this book and you are from somewhere else, this knowledge is also for you.

Gardening is a skill, and like any skill, it can be learned. Gardening takes time before you see the fruits of your work, but if you are consistent and persevere, it will yield results. Therefore, if you've never dared to grow anything, or you've tried and did not succeed the first time, or you think you don't have time, or space, or means, this book is for you.

Chapter 1:
Initial Considerations

A garden, like any enterprise that you embark on, requires a good amount of initial thinking. There are a series of factors that you have to consider prior to getting your hands dirty that are key to the success of any garden, no matter its size or the type of crops that we wish to grow.

In this initial chapter, we will take a look at the making of a garden: placement, soil considerations, design, and other factors to ensure that your vegetable garden has a strong foundation.

Space

Where to Put Your Vegetable Garden

The first thing to consider in any garden is the location. How do we decide where to plant? Can it be done anywhere? There is not a single answer to this, but there are certain requirements that you should take into consideration when evaluating the best location.

Exposure to Sunlight

Sunlight is one of the most important things to consider when choosing the location of your garden. Most vegetables need at least six hours of unobstructed sunlight (what we call "full sun"), or even up to eight hours, if possible. Some crops can work with having less exposure ("partial sun" or "partial shade") but, in general, the more sun your garden receives the more your crops will thrive.

The area where you live will have an impact in determining if your garden requires additional structures related to sunlight. A colder climate might demand a cold frame which allows plants to be in direct sunlight but to escape the dangers of frost. The harsh sun of a warmer climate could require some form of shading to avoid loss of moisture or burning.

Water Accessibility

Plants need water, that is no secret. However, sometimes we underestimate how crucial the distance to the water source is when choosing a location to plant: The closer, the better. Water is heavy, and transporting bucket after bucket under the harsh sun will most likely drain the joy out of tending for your plants. A closer outlet from where you can water with a hose or from where it's not tiresome to carry a bucket or watering can would be ideal.

The soil type of your garden will have a big impact on the watering schedule: Dry soil will require more water and will retain less moisture, so keep this in mind when planning the watering of the garden.

Protection From the Wind

Depending on the location of your garden and the kind of crops that you want to produce, you might need to consider a wind barrier. Harsh winds can dry the soil and topple upright crops and climbing vegetables, while drier winds can suck the moisture out of the plants or cause wind burn.

Building a solid fence or planting near a wall might also have a negative effect. Gusts of wind get trapped and, without an escape, create small turbulences that will damage crops. Hedges or woven fences are ideal, as they act as a barrier while allowing the wind to escape.

Soil Quality

The quality of your soil is important to determine what kind of terrain preparation you will have to do, unless you are planning to use containers or raised beds. As a first step, you can observe the state of your lawn: A healthy, lush lawn most likely will indicate good soil.

Rich, loamy soil is composed of equal parts sand and silt, with a smaller amount of clay. If you happen to have an unbalanced soil, you will have to amend it by adding organic matter: Too much sand will drain water faster, drying the soil, and too much clay will retain excess moisture, suffocating the roots.

Level Ground/Gentle Slope

Ideally, a vegetable garden should be placed either on a level ground or on a gentle slope, avoiding low spots that might gather water when it rains. If your only available place is on a not-so-gentle slope, it's better to plant at the top (cold pockets are more likely to form at the bottom of the slope) but taking the wind into account.

Effort

Gardening can be a very demanding activity, so when you are planning your garden, you should consider how much effort and time you are able and willing to invest: How much will it take for you to tear out the grass and loosen the soil? Are there rocks that need to be removed? Should you build walls or install raised beds? Or should you use containers instead?

The desired size of your garden and the type of crops that you want to keep are also key elements when thinking about effort: When in doubt, it's always better to start small and build your way up!

Small Space Vegetable Gardening Tips

Ways to Utilize Small Spaces

Contrary to what some people think, you don't need a ton of space to have a garden. As long as you have a small sunny spot, you can grow produce in patios, yards, balconies and even windowsills. There are, of course, some things that you will have to take into consideration.

Layout Considerations

Small gardens will require the same basic considerations of any garden: six hours of sunlight (if not possible, you can still grow partial shade crops like lettuce, leafy greens, roots or others), appropriate watering, and good soil. However, unlike big gardens, they don't have enough room for rotating crops and are more susceptible to pests and fungal diseases. You will need to be attentive to combat them.

Types of Small Gardens

The small space will not only reduce the number of plants that you can grow but will also crowd different crops next to each other. It's better to choose plants that grow well together, pairing tall plants next to smaller ones that can grow in partial shade, choosing varieties that reduce infestations, and planting slow-growing plants next to others that grow faster.

As you prioritize which plants to grow, consider what kind of vegetables you use more, which are harder to come by in your area, and which ones are expensive at the market but can be grown without major difficulties.

When purchasing plants or seeds for a small garden look out for compact varieties (usually the tags or labels will tell you the size of the mature plant) which are bred to be smaller. You can also plant your vegetables and herbs next to your flowers, which will attract pollinators.

Vertical gardens are another solution to reduced spaces: There are many vegetable varieties, like beans, pumpkins, and tomatoes, that can be trained to climb onto a structure to avoid the bulkiness of their bush variations. For more climbing crop ideas, check Chapter 3: Vegetables and Fruits on a Vine.

Lastly, you have to consider that quick-growing plants (like lettuce or beans) yield a lot of produce in a short amount of time, but the plant also exhausts itself faster. Planting young plants next to mature ones (succession planting) guarantees that you will have a replacement ready to go when the older plants stop producing.

Growing Fruits and Vegetables in Containers

Planting in containers allows for more control of sun exposure, soil, and of growing conditions in general. Most (if not all) crops can be grown in containers, provided that the pot is the right size for the mature plant, but you should take into consideration that the type of container will affect the needs of the plant. For example, clay or terracotta pots lose moisture quicker than plastic ones, and the darker the color of the container, the more heat it will retain.

Windowsill Gardens

Windowsill gardens are not only a solution to limited space, but also a way to have your plants and herbs within easy reach and to grow them indoors. This will protect them from the frost and the wind and will allow you to grow seasonal vegetables all year round.

Soils

Know Your Garden Soil: How to Make the Most of Your Soil Type

Soil is not merely the place where your crops are planted, but it's also the element that provides the nutrients, water, and air that they need for their proper development. Each type of soil has its own blend of nutrients and minerals that determine which plants will thrive there.

Having a specific type of soil in your area doesn't mean that you will have to forgo growing certain crops. The ideal environment for any plant can be created: in containers and raised beds, by filling them with balanced soil catered to your needs, in big gardens and landscapes, by adding to existing soil the elements that it lacks.

Six Types of Soil

Clay Soil

Clay soil tends to be compact when dry and lumpy when wet, has few air spaces and drains poorly. However, it's rich in nutrients. With enhanced drainage, it's an excellent medium for cultivating.

What to grow: Perennials, shrubs, fruit trees, ornamental trees, summer vegetables.

Sandy Soil

Sandy soil is gritty and easy to cultivate. It drains well, dries fast, and retains heat, but good drainage also means that the water can wash nutrients out of the soil, a problem that can be fixed by adding organic amendments and mulch.

What to grow: Shrubs and bulbs, root crops, lettuce, strawberries, peppers, corn, squash, zucchini, collard greens, tomatoes.

Silty Soil

Silty soil is soft, rich in nutrients, and can be easily cultivated and compacted. It holds moisture very well, but it needs help with drainage. This can be done through the addition of organic matter.

What to grow: Moisture-loving trees (like willow, cypress, or birch), shrubs, climbers, grasses, perennials. Most vegetables and fruits will thrive with the proper drainage.

Peaty Soil

Peaty soil is dark, damp, and spongy. It's acidic, which slows the decomposition of organic matter, making peaty soil low on nutrients. It heats up fast and holds water, so it needs help draining. With the addition of organic matter, compost and lime, or soil amendments, the acidity can be reduced, and the drainage improved.

What to grow: Shrubs, vegetables like brassicas, legumes, root crops, and salad crops.

Chalky Soil

Chalky soil has a large grain and it's mixed with rocks. It has good drainage. It is alkaline, so it needs fertilizers and a balanced pH. Adding humus helps with water retention and makes it easier to work with.

What to grow: Trees, bulbs and shrubs, vegetables like spinach, beets, sweet corn, or cabbage.

Loamy Soil

Loamy soil is the most balanced type of soil, containing a good mix of sand, silt, and clay. It drains very well while retaining the right amount of moisture. It is nutrient rich and is easy to cultivate. Due to its acidity, it can benefit from the addition of organic matter.

Loamy soil is the most productive type of soil, but it can easily become depleted of nutrients or dry out. You can help keep its vitality by rotating crops, adding compost, or using mulch.

What to grow: Climbers, perennials, shrubs and tubers, most vegetables and berry crops.

Simple Tests to Determine Your Soil Type

There are several ways in which you can determine what kind of soil you have. Knowing this will allow you to make the necessary amendments to ensure that your crops will have the proper growing conditions.

Squeeze Test

Grab a handful of soil and squeeze it. Clay soil will be sticky, slick to the touch, and will hold its shape, while sandy soil will feel gritty and crumble easily. Peaty soil will feel spongy. Both loamy and silty soil will be smooth and will hold shape for a short period of time.

Settle Test

Add water and a small amount of soil to a transparent container. Shake it and let it rest for about 12 hours.

- Clay/Silty soil: cloudy water, a layer of particles at the bottom
- Sandy soil: clear water, a layer of particles at the bottom
- Peaty soil: slightly cloudy water, particles floating on the surface
- Chalky soil: pale gray water and white, gritty fragments at the bottom
- Loamy soil: clear water, with the thicker particles at the bottom and the finer particles at the top

Acid Test

Soil pH tends to range between 4.0 and 8.5, but plants will thrive on soils that have a pH of 6.5 to 7: At this level the soil is rich in nutrients and minerals. The best way of determining your soil pH is through a pH test kit, which can be purchased online or at most garden centers. You should also consider that areas with soft water tend to have more acidic soil, while in areas with hard water the soil is more alkaline.

Soil Test Kit

This kind of kit will allow you to assess the pH levels and the primary nutrients (N-P-K) of your soil. It's recommended that you test your soil periodically during the growing season. This will allow you to fertilize your garden in a more strategic and economic way, targeting the specific needs of your soil.

How to Make the Most of Your Soil, Whatever the Type

Plants thrive in neutral soil, but some will do very well in more acidic or alkaline soil. That is not to say that you can't plant in that soil. Whatever its type, you can adjust, temporarily, the pH values through additives to cater to the needs of your desired crops.

If you need to make your soil more alkaline, you can do this by adding ground lime. For a more acidic medium, you can mix the soil with aluminum sulfate or sulfur.

Very alkaline soils, as well as soils low in nutrients, will benefit from the addition of organic matter such as manure or compost, and from organic mulch (straw, dried grass, leaves, etc.), that will incorporate into the soil as it decays.

Organic matter will also be of help in clay soils. Mixed in large quantities during the fall, it will help aerate and loosen the soil. This can also be done by adding greensand.

Make Sure Your Soil is Healthy

You should think of your soil as a living thing. It needs water, food and air. There are three main nutrients that it needs: Nitrogen, phosphorus, and potassium (N-P-K), that are usually added through organic matter. Nitrogen helps with the growth of strong leaves and stems and will help with the dark green coloring of crops like broccoli, cabbage, or lettuce. Phosphorus is essential in root and early plant growth, blossoms and developing fruit, and it's crucial in crops that develop from pollinated flowers, like tomatoes, cucumbers, or squash. Lastly, potassium aids with root vigor, provides resistance to disease and stress, and helps enhance the flavor.

After harvest, the soil is low on nutrients and needs to be renewed. One way of doing this is by planting cover crops (like legumes, buckwheat, vetch, or clover) that will restore the nitrogen of the soil, aerate it, and add organic matter. These crops are tilled into the soil before they reach maturity, and they quickly decompose and integrate into the soil in time for planting season.

Rotating your crops, planting cover crops, using green manure (fresh crops incorporated into the soil) and mulch, or adding compost and fertilizer are tried and true ways of restoring the soil's health and nutrients.

Phosphorus levels can be improved through the addition of rock phosphate (or rock dust), while the incorporation of living organisms like the fungus Mycorrhizae can aid the plants to better absorb water and nutrients. Adding worms also can speed the composting process and help spread the fertilizer.

Tips for Improving Your Garden's Soil Quality

Having good soil is not enough to ensure healthy crops. A good, prepared soil is crucial, and it will be the foundation of a successful harvest.

Spring Soil Prep

Once you have decided where to plant your garden, you have to start prepping the soil. You can do this by following three easy steps.

1) Start by clearing out the soil: Remove the rocks and debris and dig up the grass. Clear out any weeds.
2) Loosen the soil: Try to loosen soil to a depth of 8 to 12 inches to ensure that the roots will not have problems developing.
3) Add organic matter: To moist (not wet) soil add two to three inches of compost or aged manure.

Improving Your Soil

Soil Amendments

Soil amendments are added to the existing soil to improve the soil's texture, the nutrient content, or the pH level.

Organic Soil Amendments

- Plant material: Straw, grass, or leaves that are decomposed and mixed into the soil several months before planting.
- Compost: Decayed plant material that is worked into the soil a few weeks prior to planting to add nutrients and lower the pH
- Leaf Mold: Decomposed leaves that add nutrients and structure

- Aged Manure: Soil conditioner. Must be added weeks before planting. Never add fresh manure to a vegetable garden, as it might introduce diseases into the soil.
- Coconut Coir: Soil conditioner that helps retain water.
- Bark, woodchips, sawdust: Must be composted before adding them into the soil. Added fresh, they will absorb the nitrogen of the soil.
- Topsoil: soil replacement that is added with other amendments to increase volume.
- Wood Ash: Raises the pH of acidic soils. Only use it when recommended by a soil test.

Inorganic Soil Amendments

- Sulfur: Lowers the pH of alkaline soils. Only use it when recommended by a soil test.
- Lime: Raises the pH of acidic soils. Only use when recommended by a soil test.
- Perlite: Helps aerate compost and retains water. Helps container plants with drainage.
- Vermiculite: Aerates the soil and retains water and nutrients, releasing them over time.
- Sand: Helps loosen compact soils and helps with drainage.

Amending with Organic Matter

There are several benefits gained from the addition of organic matter into your garden's soil. Organic matter loosens compact soils, like clay soil, and improves drainage and aeration. It releases minerals and helps with water and nutrient retention, especially in fast-draining soils like sandy soil. It makes compact soils easier to work with and helps adjust the pH. It's a natural slow-release fertilizer and it's also a source of food for beneficial organisms that live in the soil, like fungi, insects, earthworms, and other beneficial bacteria.

Fixing Different Soil Types

- Sandy or Chalky Soils: These types of soils dry very quickly and don't readily retain nutrients. This can be helped with the addition of three to four inches of organic matter during the preparation of your soil (in subsequent years add only one to two inches), and the use of mulch to retain moisture. Cover crops can help to improve the structure of the soil.
- Clay or Peaty Soils: These kinds of soils retain excess water and are very compact, often making them difficult to work with. This can be helped with the addition of three to four inches of organic matter during the preparation of your soil (in subsequent years add only one to two inches). Fibrous organic matter like straw or bark mulch will improve the structure of the soil. You should never add sand to this type of soil: It will worsen the situation, making the soil even harder.
- Silty Soil: This type of soil is susceptible to erosion, which can be helped by adding one inch of organic matter every year and avoiding tilling.
- Loamy Soil: The more balanced soil, loamy soil generally doesn't need amendments, but if a soil test determines a lack of nutrients, it can benefit from the use of organic matter.

Remember that more organic matter doesn't necessarily mean more benefits: Too much can increase the number of microorganisms that can affect both nutrients and pH. Organic matter should never be more than a quarter of your soil mixture.

How to Add Organic Matter

Ideally, you would add organic matter in the fall, and it would decompose by spring. If you are not able to do this, you can still add it in spring as soon as the soil is workable. Check the workability by grabbing a handful of soil (not from the top, dig a few inches) and trying to form a ball. If the ball crumbles or falls apart, the soil is dry enough. If it retains its shape, it's too wet and you should wait a few days and try again.

As soon as the soil is workable you can add the organic matter in the following steps:

1) Add a two- to four-inch layer of organic matter and mix it into the soil with the help of a garden fork until it's well combined.
2) Water well and check the moisture of the soil.
3) Wait at least two weeks to plant.
4) Before planting, remove any sticks or rocks from the surface and rake the soil to level it.
5) Avoid stepping into newly amended soil or you will compact it.
6) Add organic matter every season to maintain the soil.

A Note on Raised Beds

When talking about raised beds we usually think about a box or frame with no top or bottom, sitting on top of the ground. Raised beds can also be a mound of soil (six to eight inches high) above ground. Raised beds help with erosion and weeds and they give you more control over the soil. They are also helpful in colder climates: You can help the soil retain heat by covering the bed with something light blocking and non-porous like a dark plastic sheet.

Designing and Planting

Zones

The US Department of Agriculture (USDA) has developed a system to determine which plants will better survive and grow in each area of the United States of America. This system is updated regularly and divides the territory into 11 zones by their minimum average annual temperature.

Hardiness Zones

What do Hardiness Zones Mean?

Each hardiness zone represents a difference of 10°F and is subdivided into regions A and B (each one representing a difference of 5°F). The term "hardiness" refers to the ability of each plant to survive cold temperatures.

As with any system, the hardiness zone system has its flaws. For example, it doesn't account for factors like precipitation, elevation, or snow.

How to Use Hardiness Zones Information

A better understanding of the hardiness zones will help you to pick which plants have a better chance of surviving the winter in your zone. You should take your zone into consideration when you are choosing perennials, trees, or shrubs, as these plants will have to endure numerous winters.

First, you need to know in which hardiness zone you are located, as this will give you the minimum average temperature of your region. Then, when picking the plants for your garden, you need to be aware of their ability to withstand the cold. This information can usually be found on the plant's tags (if you are buying it from a nursery), or you can check the USDA's recommendations for each crop.

Once you find a crop suitable for your Hardiness Zone, look into the climate aspects that the hardiness zones system doesn't take into consideration. For example, how does that crop withstand the average maximum heat of your region? Do you live in a microclimate (a small area that has a different climate than the surrounding area) that is not accounted for in the system? Will your regional levels of precipitation or the altitude affect that crop?

If you are just dipping your toes into gardening and want to play it safe, you can start by choosing crops that are rated hardy for one zone higher and one zone lower than yours. This way you will make sure to account for any unexpected fluctuation in the weather.

Designing

Designing a Vegetable Garden

How Large Should It Be?

As a beginner it's always better to start small and build your way up than to try to tackle a huge garden from the start. Unless you are considering crops that take up a lot of space, like corn, you could start with a space around 12 x 20 feet. You can plan the space taking into consideration a possible future expansion of the garden.

Digging the Garden

Once you have an idea of the size of the garden and where your beds will be, the first step is to measure and mark the perimeter, the beds, and the paths.

Remove grass and weeds with a sharp, flat-edged spade. If you start prepping the soil during the fall, you can till the site but not remove the grass, leaving it there to serve as compost. In the spring there will be a few weeds that will need pulling out.

If digging and removing the sod is too much of an effort, you can always plant on top of it, provided you have good soil. You will need to put a thick layer of newspaper (around 8 to 10 sheets) on the ground, wet it and add four to six inches of good soil. The paper will smother the grass and weeds, eventually decomposing and integrating into the soil. On the other hand, if your soil needs amendments, it's better to remove the sod to make space for them and to better integrate them into the soil.

Planning

Using a bed system will help you to plan, grow, and harvest with ease. It will also make it easier to protect the plants and to group together similar crops. You can have soil level beds, edging beds (beds with a border around them), or raised beds. You should be able to reach the center of the bed without overstretching.

Another thing that you should take into consideration when planning your beds is that tall plants should be placed farthest away from the sun so they don't shade over lower crops. Also, commonly used plants that don't need rotation (like herbs) should be placed closest to the entrance.

How you plan your garden is entirely up to you, but each style has its pros and cons:

- Rows: The neat and tidy rows of this style are ideal for good air circulation, make weeding and harvesting easier, and avoid soil compaction, which leads to healthier roots. The downside of this style is that it takes up a lot of space. Also, tall plants that tend to flop will need to be trellised.
- Wide rows: This style calls for long blocks of the same crops, which takes less space than single rows. The closeness of the plants functions like mulch, helping with water retention and smothering the weeds.

  This style is not ideal for all crops, as there are plants (tomatoes, for example) that do not do well when crowded. You should also be careful in very humid areas, as the crowding of the plants can exacerbate problems like rotting or excess water retention.

- Four-Square: Originally this style consisted of four equal, slightly raised beds with narrow paths in between, but you can divide the garden however you like to better fit your needs. The raised beds help with drainage and make it easier for the soil to warm up in spring, while guaranteeing that you will never walk on top of the soil. The compartments make for an easier crop rotation, and you can have a specific section for perennials.

  The downside of this style is its semi-permanent structure. If you want to move part of the garden or make it bigger it will take more effort than other structures.

- Eclectic: This style is free-form, and a mix of different styles. It is very ornamental, and very easy to fit into an existing garden, as you plant wherever you have an available space. The combination of vegetable crops with flowers has the advantage of attracting more pollinators and helping with pest control but the lack of clear division makes it more difficult to maintain, weed, and harvest.
- Creating paths: You can create paths in any of the styles that we have described. They can be simply grass paths or they can be made of mulch over cardboard, gravel, bricks, or pavers. You should prioritize having easily navigable paths that allow you to comfortably tend to your beds, haul manure and compost, and harvest. Your paths should be wide enough to fit a wheelbarrow or a cart, should you need them.

Weather

Weather and Gardening

When looking at the tags and descriptions of plants, you will come across words like annual, perennial, tropical, etc. These kinds of words are used to describe the characteristics of the different crops and how they respond to weather conditions like light, temperature, wind, rainfall, or if they grow for just one season or come back year after year.

How do I Utilize Weather and Climate Information for Successful Gardening?

You can't control the weather but understanding how it affects your area will allow you to pick the plants better suited for your garden. Also, if you are set on crops that need different conditions, you will be able to plan for protection from the elements to ensure the survival of your plants.

How Does the Weather Affect my Garden?

Weather has a direct effect on the survival of plants and is, next to soil and plant care, the ultimate factor for plants to thrive. Plants favor certain places to grow due to climate (how the weather in your area behaves over time), so being aware of your area's climate is key to ensure a successful garden.

What are the Key Weather Elements for Gardening?

Extremely low temperatures can instantly kill your plants if they are not suited for it, or they are not properly protected. The USDA's system of hardiness zones will help you in the selection of proper crops. This book focuses on zones 7, 8 and 9 specifically, so check your USDA zone's directives if you are from a different zone.

- Freeze is classified according to the effects it might have on vegetation:
    - Light freeze: 29° to 32°F (-1.7° to 0°C). It will likely kill tender plants.
    - Moderate freeze: 25° to 28°F (-3.9° to -2.2°C). It will be widely destructive to most vegetation.

    - Severe freeze: -24°F (-4.4°C). It will cause severe damage.
- Frost dates: In combination with the USDA's hardiness zones, it is helpful to be aware of your local frost dates. Frost dates are the average date from the last light freeze of spring to the first light freeze of fall. These dates are an estimate based on historical data, so frost has a slight chance of occurring outside of the given dates.

  Being aware of your local frost dates and consulting your local weather forecast will allow you to protect your plants from incoming frost.
- Heat: While extreme high temperatures will not instantly kill your crops, they will stress them and eventually wilt them. The American Horticultural Society (AHS) has a Heat Zones system that can help you when selecting the proper plants for your area.
- Wind: Wind exacerbates transpiration in plants (loss of water vapor) and water evaporation from the soil, which can lead to moisture loss. In combination with high temperatures, it can result in plant dehydration. You can reduce the circulation of air in extremely windy areas with fences and hedges.
- Moisture: Water is essential for every plant, even for those advertised as "drought tolerant." Excess water can also be prejudicial—soggy soil can decrease the oxygen supply to plant roots. Knowing your local rainfall and drought seasons will help you to know when your plants might need

additional water and which plants are susceptible to drowning.

Fertilizers

What is Fertilizer?

Besides having soil rich in organic matter, crops will sometimes need fertilizer to get proper nutrition. When you harvest your crops, these plants have absorbed nutrients from the soil during the growing season. If you plant again in that depleted soil, the new crops will not have enough nutrients to grow properly. Fertilizer is added to replace those nutrients.

Fertilizer, either natural or artificial, is a substance that contains the essential nutrients that plants need to properly develop and thrive.

Like we saw with soil amendments and water, an excess of fertilizer will do more harm than good, so you will need to be careful not to over fertilize.

When to Fertilize Your Garden

Fertilizer is usually added in the spring before planting to ensure that the plants will have enough nutrients during their growth period. You can still fertilize after planting, but only in granular form, as liquid fertilizer can harm young roots.

Perennials should also be fertilized at the beginning of spring, around the date of the last frost. The soil will be warm enough to properly absorb the nutrients, but there won't be new growth that could be damaged by the fertilizer.

While spring application is the general rule when talking about fertilizers, each crop has a slightly different growth period, so knowing the particular characteristics of your different crops will be helpful when fertilizing.

Always Take a Soil Test

Soil tests are the only certain way of determining the state of the nutrients of your soil, but you don't need to test every year. If you test your soil and build it up accordingly the first time, in the coming years you can maintain it with smaller amounts of fertilizer.

How Much of What Kind of Fertilizer Should I Use?

Fertilizer labels will have a combination of three numbers, corresponding to the amount of nitrogen, phosphorus, and potassium (N-P-K) in each mix. These numbers refer to the percentage of weight of each nutrient that is mixed with the filler. The label will also instruct you the amount of fertilizer to use per 1000 square feet.

For starters, a balanced, general vegetable fertilizer (for example, a 10-10-10) will do. If you are keen on growing specific crops, you can look into their particular needs and purchase a fertilizer mix catered to those crops.

Processed vs. Organic Fertilizers

Processed fertilizers (also called synthetic or chemical) are made from natural ingredients that have been refined to be more concentrated. They usually have a quick-release format and are water soluble.

On the other hand, plant-derived organic fertilizers generally come in granular form. They are spread over the soil and mixed in and they have a slower release. They tend to be more expensive than processed fertilizers, but the slow-release format means that you don't need to apply them as often.

The nutritional values don't differ from one format to another. Using a slow-release fertilizer would be ideal to ensure a proper absorption of the nutrients but is not always necessary.

How to Apply Granular Fertilizers

To apply granulated fertilizer, apply the indicated amount over non-cultivated soil and mix with the top three to five inches. Mix it with a spade or hoe, and then water to ensure that it's correctly distributed. If you have already planted, you can spread it alongside the rows and water or gently mix it in, being careful with the roots. If you have incoming rain, you can apply it and let the rainfall do the mixing for you.

During the growing season, add smaller amounts of fertilizer on the topsoil of the plants that require a boost. The fertilizer's label should tell you how often to apply it.

How to Apply Liquid Fertilizers

Liquid fertilizers are usually water soluble. Dilute the fertilizer according to the instructions and then apply it to the leaves and roots of the plants. Watering your plants thoroughly before fertilizing with a liquid will ensure a more even distribution and absorption.

Never apply liquid fertilizer at the same time that you plant, or on recently planted crops. New roots are vulnerable and liquid fertilizer might burn them.

If your fertilizer of choice comes in a liquid spray format, it's better to apply it during early mornings or early evenings. Avoid applying when the sun is high, or during hot days to avoid burning the leaves.

Composting

What is Composting

Composting is the process of recycling organic matter (like food scraps, clippings, leaves, etc.) into fertilizer by speeding up their natural decomposition. This is done by providing an ideal environment where decomposing organisms like bacteria, fungi, and bugs can do their work. The resulting matter is rich in nutrients. While big composting facilities do exist, this process can easily be done at home.

Benefits of Composting

Composting can reduce the amount of waste that we discard at home and that would end up being processed and sent to a landfill. Home composting also reduces the amount of methane gas produced by landfills and is a way to reduce food waste, a prevalent problem in the US.

Composted matter contains the main nutrients needed for healthy crops, such as nitrogen, phosphorus, potassium, and other minerals like calcium, iron, and magnesium, while being free from the chemicals that are present in processed fertilizers. Fertilizing with compost also increases the soil’s capacity for water retention, aiding moisture retention and reducing the amount of water needed in agricultural practices.

Types of Home Composting

You can compost both indoors and outdoors, but your approach to it will depend on your available space, how much waste you produce, what kind of waste you produce, and how much time you can spend on the process.

- Cold composting: Also known as passive composting, cold composting is an easy, but slow, way to compost. You just need to let nature do its job. This method is ideal if you have little waste and you are not in a hurry for finished compost, as it can take months for the compost to be finished. Another downside to this method is that it can sometimes develop harmful bacteria, in addition to being smellier than hot composting.
- Hot composting: Also known as active composting, this is a faster and more managed method that requires you to keep the carbon and nitrogen at an appropriate level for decomposing the organic waste. Done correctly, it can take as little as a month, depending on the amount of waste, and the temperature of the pile will eliminate any harmful bacteria or weed seeds.

Hot compost needs to be kept at a temperature of 130° to 140°F to allow the decomposing organisms to work faster. You can check the temperature with a thermometer or by simply sticking your hand into the compost pile. If the heat is uncomfortable, it means it is working.

You need to monitor the temperature regularly. When the pile temperature dips below 130°F, it is time to turn it. The aeration will cause the microbial organisms in the pile to restart the decomposition process which, in turn, will cause the temperature to rise again.

The other key element of hot composting is moisture: Your pile should be neither wet nor dry, just moist.

Done properly, your hot compost pile should be ready to be used in around three weeks.

How to Compost

Decomposition of organic waste has four main elements: nitrogen, carbon, air, and water. The ideal ratio is 25 to 30 parts of carbon to one-part nitrogen, but a good rule of thumb when home composting is two to four parts brown material for every one-part green. Too much carbon will dry the pile and slow the process, while too much nitrogen will make it excessively wet and smelly.

- Nitrogen rich matter (greens): fresh organic material like food scraps, coffee grounds, and fresh grass clippings
- Carbon rich matter (browns): dead leaves and clippings, branches, twigs, and paper
- Oxygen: If you are cold composting, you do not have to worry about airflow or moisture. If you prefer hot compost, you can ensure a good air flow by layering your materials in small pieces and regularly turning the piles. Aeration needs to be consistent to reduce smells and speed up the process. You should turn your piles once a week during summer and once a month during winter. You can also add large sticks or piping to the piles to ensure a proper airflow.
- Water: When hot composting, your piles will have to be moist (not wet). If you are adding food waste

to the compost it will be wet enough, but you can always add water if it is too dry. If it is too wet, adding browns will help.

- The optimal temperature for composting is 130° to 140°F.

The ideal size for a compost pile or bin is around a 3-foot cube. Larger piles will have problems with aeration and will be harder to turn. Additionally, remember that the smaller the pieces of waste, the better they will decompose.

Your compost should be placed somewhere dry and shady. In humid, rainier climates place it on a spot with good drainage to avoid the pile from getting soggy. If you live in a sunny area, make sure to place it in the shade to prevent it from drying.

How to Start Your Compost:

Add alternating thin layers of browns and greens, making sure to end with a layer of browns on top. If needed, you can wet the pile as you layer. Once built, leave it untouched for a few days to allow decomposition to begin. After four or five days, start turning it and monitoring the moisture levels.

Which Compost Bin Should You Use?

There are different types of bins that can be used for composting, and you can pick any of them that better suits your needs.

- Closed bins are good at retaining heat and moisture. They usually have an open bottom and are placed directly on top of the soil. This type of bin is easy to build from a wine crate, a garbage can, a storage bin, wood pallets, etc., if you'd rather not buy one. Depending on the material, you might have to add a removable top and punch holes on the sides to ensure good airflow.

- Open bins require less maintenance, and work best with yard waste as food waste might attract animals. An open bin can consist of just a pile on the ground, with or without something simple like a perimeter of chicken wire to act as an enclosure: They are easy to build.
- Tumbler bins are sealed containers that can be rotated with a handle, making it easy to aerate and mix the waste. They speed up the composting process, but they are very difficult to build yourself.

Trench Composting

Trench composting is a method of composting where you bury waste directly in the ground. It helps with water conservation and it's odorless and invisible. You must simply dig a hole, fill it with organic waste, and cover it up with the soil, letting nature do the rest. As long as you can comfortably dig, you can use this method all year long. While very hands free, this method is not practical on an ongoing basis, unless you have the space to regularly dig up holes in your yard.

Another benefit of trench composting is that it allows you to include cooked food waste, meat, dairy, and grains in the mix. Being buried, there is a smaller chance of attracting animals, provided that the waste is buried deep (at least 12 inches).

To build a trench compost pit you will have to dig a hole 12 to 24 inches deep, fill it with your waste, make sure that it is moist, and cover it back up. It will take a longer time to decompose, and you will not be able to harvest the finished product, so you should build the pit where you want to add the resulting nutrients. If you have less waste (or space), you can dig multiple smaller holes of the same depth, but make sure you mark them to avoid digging on the same spot.

A few useful tips:

- Do not build a trench-composting pit near other plants to avoid harming or infecting them.
- As the matter decomposes, the top of the trench will sink, so avoid planting on top of it during the process.
- In arid areas, water the trench to ensure moisture retention.

Vermicomposting

Also known as worm composting, vermicomposting is a method that can be done either outdoors or indoors year-round. Its product is odorless and nutrient rich. It's very low maintenance, as the most effort it requires is the collection of the compost every few months.

You can either buy or make a worm composter yourself. A simple bin with holes on the sides and bottom will do. It will need to be raised from the ground to allow for the flow of liquid. Fill it with worm bedding (brown materials like shredded paper or cardboard, dry leaves, or straw) and soil.

The ideal type of worms for vermicomposting are red wigglers. They require little maintenance and prefer the compost environment. An at-home vermicomposting system will need no more than a pound of worms to function properly.

Once a week, feed the worms by mixing waste (such as vegetable and fruit peels, stems and leaves, crushed egg shells, dead plants, grass clippings, feathers and hair, roots, and seeds) with their bedding. Avoid feeding them animal products, fats and oils, and thick food scraps like corn cobs. Also, don't feed them onion and garlic waste if you want to avoid a smelly worm bin, and excess citrus to prevent the soil from being too acidic. Check regularly that the soil is moist.

A few useful tips:

- Do not use metal bins for vermicomposting, as it can increase the temperature of the environment.
- While you can build a vermicomposting system outdoors, an indoor location is ideal to ensure that the worms will not suffer from extreme temperature changes.
- Do not overfeed the worms the first few days. Give them time to adjust to the environment and to better determine how much waste they require. Remember that they will need to be fed once a week.

What Not to Compost

At home you can compost anything that comes from the ground, from grass clippings to cardboard. However, you should avoid some things that, though compostable by themselves, can attract animals and insects, or leave pathogens in your soil.

You should never compost:

- Pet waste and litter: It contains parasites and bacteria that can be harmful if ingested. The USDA has a protocol to compost dog waste at home, but the composted product can't be applied to crops.
- Black walnut tree leaves and twigs, coal, or charcoal ash: might release substances that are harmful to plants.
- Plants that are ridden with insects or disease: might infect other plants.
- Dairy products, eggs, fats, grease, lard, oils, meat and fish bones or scraps: might create odor problems, attract pests, and carry pathogens.
- Trimmings and clippings treated with chemical pesticides: though less dangerous, the chemical residues might kill the beneficial bacteria in your compost.
- Inorganic material: plastic, glossy or colored paper.

Safety Precautions

Remember that compost is decomposing matter, so handle the waste carefully, making sure to wash your hands and avoid touching your face.

To reduce the chance of fruit flies, bury the greens under a layer of browns, and make sure that your compost is not too wet. Boiling your food scraps before composting can also help. You can also keep a compost container in your kitchen and only add the waste to the pile when it's full.

How to Use Compost

Compost needs to mature before you can use it to fertilize your crops. Immature compost can damage your plants and attract rodents and pests. Mature compost will have a crumbly and smooth texture, with no recognizable bits, and it should be dark in color. It should smell like earth. If it smells sour or like ammonia, it means it's immature. The original size of your compost pile should have been reduced by a third.

Once you are sure your compost is mature and ready to use, you can use it as mulch, add it to potting soil or crop beds, distribute it on your lawn, or add it to potted plants and fruit trees.

Mature compost will not go bad, but it can dry, get too wet, or get old. You can still use old compost, but the nutrient level will have diminished.

Rabbit and Chicken Manure

Though using pet waste as a fertilizer is not recommended, chicken and rabbit manure can be an exception, provided that they are handled with care and that the crops fertilized with that manure are thoroughly washed before consuming. People prone to foodborne illnesses (young children, pregnant women, persons with cancer, diabetes, liver issues, etc.) should not consume uncooked vegetables or fruits from gardens composted with manure.

Rabbit Manure

Unlike other types of animal waste, rabbit manure doesn't need to be composted to be used. It can be added to a compost pile as a booster and its pellet form makes for easy application to the soil and crop beds. It's also richer in N-P-K than other types of animal manure.

Chicken Manure

Though chicken manure can be safely used as vegetable fertilizer, it does require composting to avoid it from burning the plants and to destroy any possible pathogens. Chicken litter is a mix of feces, urine, feathers, and bedding material. When properly aged and composted, it's an excellent soil amendment with high N-P-K values.

For proper composting, the compost pile must have adequate drainage and must be turned once a week to ensure proper aeration and to prevent foul odors. Another option is to dry age the manure before adding it to the pile by spreading it thinly over a tarp under the sun.

Unlike rabbit manure, chicken manure should only be added as a soil amendment at least 3 months before harvest, and it should never be added directly on top of the beds of already growing vegetables.

Planting Your Garden

When it comes to planting the crops, you have several ways to go: You can start from zero by planting seeds in trays and pots, or directly into the soil, or you can get small plants that are ready to be transplanted directly into the garden beds. The basic care of the plants will be the same, but the planting method might vary depending on your intended crop and the climate of your area.

Planting Seeds

If you decide to start growing from seed, your method of choice will mostly be determined by seed size.

Small Seeds

Seed trays are ideal for planting small seeds. Fill the tray with soil and slightly flatten it. Watering the soil before planting will ensure that the seeds won't be washed away later.

Sprinkle the seeds as evenly as you can on top of the surface. If the seeds are clumped together, they won't grow properly. Cover the tray with a layer of vermiculite or with plastic (with holes to ensure air flow) to insulate them. Do not forget to label the tray.

Once the plants are grown to three or four inches tall, as a general rule, you can move them to small pots or to the garden soil.

Large Seeds

Large seeds are easier to plant, so you can plant directly in individual pots. Fill them with soil, make a small hole, plant the seed, and cover it with soil or compost. Water lightly and cover the pots to insulate them.

Direct Sow

Some vegetables, like cabbages and carrots, can be sown directly into the garden beds. For this method, the soil needs to be warm and fine in consistency, to allow the roots to grow properly.

To plant the seeds, create a small depression in the soil, at the depth indicated for each vegetable. Water the soil and then sow the seeds leaving a space of one or two inches in between to avoid crowding. Cover the seeds gently with soil and cover the bed with a tarp or plastic to retain heat and to prevent the wind from disturbing the soil.

Thinning Out

This process consists in removing seedlings (young plants) from the garden bed or seed tray to avoid overcrowding as they grow. When the seedlings are about one inch tall, they should be thinned so there is a space of four inches in between each plant. This will allow the plants to grow stronger, as they will not compete for nutrients with each other.

Hardening Off

Plants planted in trays and pots will need to be acclimated to outdoor weather before transplanting them to the garden beds. When the frost season ends, take the trays and pots outside during the day and move them back inside at night for a few days before planting them. You can also slightly lower the amount of water and fertilizer you are using.

Growing Vegetable Transplants

Growing your own transplants is not a simple task. Not planting in a garden bed means you will need to be attentive to several requirements that nature handles when planting in garden beds: temperature, fertility, light, etc.

There are a lot of benefits to growing your own plant transplants instead of buying the seedlings. You can start growing ahead of the growing season, make sure that your crops are uniform, grow plants not available as seedlings in your area, and germinate difficult crops in proper conditions. However, not all crops will benefit from all the time and effort you put into growing and transplanting them, root crops and legumes, for example.

Growing Medium

It is not recommended to use topsoil as a growing medium, as it lacks proper water and nutrient retention, and does not drain well in containers. Commercial growing mediums are usually mixed with bark, moss, vermiculite, or perlite to ensure drainage, aeration, and proper water retention.

Improving Plant Efficiency

Transplant growing is an activity that demands a lot of time and effort, so being efficient is key. Some small things that can make the task easier for you are: Use containers that can hold multiple plants instead of sowing in individual pots, make your holes uniform in depth to ensure that your plants are consistent, and label to indicate species, variety, and date of planting of every crop.

Starting the Plants

There are two methods you can use to start your seedlings: sow in small pots or containers with enough space, or sow into trays or flats and later transplant into finisher containers.

Transplanting takes time and effort, and certain crops (like pumpkins or cucumbers) can be easily damaged or even die if transplanted as seedlings into finishing containers. Seeding directly into the final containers is more labor efficient.

On the other hand, tray or flat seeding is more time efficient. When sowing in containers, you will plant one to two seeds per container, then later thin out the weaker plants, leaving only one seedling per container. A tray will give you enough room to space out the seeds and reduce the need for thinning.

No matter the method you choose, remember that the soil must be kept moist and covered to maintain proper temperature.

Containers to Consider

When choosing the containers for your seedlings, there are some things to take into consideration:

- How much space do you have?
- Are you growing to sell or for your own use?
- Do you want to reuse the containers?
- How much growing space do your intended crops require?

Containers come in various models, sizes and materials:

- Compressed peat containers: They are single use, but you can plant the seedling with them, and they will disintegrate into the soil. If you keep the plant in the container without planting for a longer time, the container might break down.
- Styrofoam containers: They are long lasting, reusable, and have insulating properties that can help to maintain temperature. They will need to be washed and sanitized before reusing to ensure that no diseases or pathogens will affect new seedlings.
- Plastic containers: They are long lasting and reusable, and easier to label. They will need to be

washed and sanitized before reusing to ensure that no diseases or pathogens will affect new seedlings.

Growing Considerations

When the seedlings emerge, they will need less water and heat than when they were germinating, but they still will need moist soil and a warm atmosphere. If your plants start growing too fast and begin to stretch, you will need to ease up on water and fertilizer and check that the temperature isn't excessive. Growing seedlings also need abundant light to properly mature.

If you have sown in trays or flats and need to move the seedlings to bigger individual pots, you should do this as the first leaves are forming (around two to three weeks after sowing). Make deeper holes, as the roots are already developed, and be very careful not to damage the stems of the plant. Carefully firm the soil around the repotted seedling and water thoroughly to reduce wilting.

Before transplanting seedlings to the garden bed, remember to gradually harden them to avoid stress.

Plant Spacing and Depth

Do your vegetables have enough space to grow?

Like any living being, plants need to be fed, watered, and cared for, and they also need "personal space" to avoid competing for nutrients and to be able to stretch and grow. Each plant needs a certain amount of space and depth, but there are general rules that we can follow to avoid being overwhelmed by the many different requirements.

Square Foot Gardening and Garden Area Sizing

The traditional method of planting in rows is not very effective in small backyard gardens, as you can't plant in the paths between the rows. Square foot gardening is more space efficient because it involves planting by area. By separating your garden into square foot sections, you can sow the appropriate number of plants or seeds by section, allowing for greater crop density than a typical row, but without overcrowding.

The size of your garden is a factor in this style. Gardens larger than four feet will make it difficult for you to comfortably reach the center without having to walk into it.

Soil Depth

Depending on the crops you want to grow, you will need between 8 and 36 inches of usable soil depth. Raised beds should be at least eight inches. You should dig the soil in your garden bed to ensure that deep-growing roots will have no trouble expanding. Most crop roots will not need more than eight inches, but you should always check before planting.

You should always slightly overfill your bed because soil will compact as the water weighs it down and air pockets inside collapse. To be on the safe side, add two extra inches of soil to the top of the beds, wet it and see how much it compresses. Add more soil, if necessary.

Quality Soil = Quality Garden

The quality and care of your soil will be the key element to a successful garden. Never use unknown soil that could contain elements detrimental to your plants. When in doubt, purchased soil is better.

Space Needed for the Most Common Crops

Crop	**Space between plants**	**Space between rows**
Artichokes	18" (45 cm)	24"-36" (60-90 cm)
Asparagus	12"-18" (30-45 cm)	60" (150 cm)
Beans, bush	2"-4" (5-10 cm)	18"-24" (45-60 cm)
Beans, pole	4"-6" (10-15 cm)	30"-36" (75-90 cm)
Beets	3"-4" (7-10 cm)	12"-18" (30-45 cm)
Black-Eyed Peas	2"-4" (5-10 cm)	30"-36" (75-90 cm)
Bok Choy	6"-12" (15-30 cm)	18"-30" (43-74 cm)
Broccoli	18"-24" (45-60 cm)	36"-40" (75-100 cm)
Brussels Sprouts	24" (60 cm)	24"-36" (60-90 cm)
Cabbage	9"-12" (23-30 cm)	36"-44" (90-112)
Carrots	1"-2" (2-5 cm)	12"-18" (30-45 cm)
Cauliflower	18"-24" (45-60 cm)	18"-24" (45-60 cm)
Celery	12"-18" (30-45 cm)	24" (60 cm)
Corn	10"-15" (25-40 cm)	36"-42" (90-105 cm)
Cucumbers, ground	8"-10" (20-25 cm)	60" (1.5 mt)

Cucumbers, trellis	2”-3” (5-8 cm)	30” (75 cm)
Eggplants	18”-24” (45-60 cm)	30”-36” (75-90 cm)
Greens	10”-18” (25-45 cm)	36”-42” (90-105 cm)
Kale	12”-18” (30-45 cm)	24” (60 cm)
Lettuce	12” (30 cm)	12” (30 cm)
Onions	4”-6” (10-15 cm)	4”-6” (10-15 cm)
Parsnips	8”-10” (20-25 cm)	18”-24” (45-60 cm)
Peas	1”-2” (2-5 cm)	18”-24” (45-60 cm)
Peppers	14”-18” (35-45 cm)	18”-24” (45-60 cm)
Potatoes	8”-12” (20-30 cm)	30”-36” (75-90 cm)
Pumpkins	60”-72” (1.5-1.8 mts)	120”-180” (3-4.5 mts)
Radishes	0.5”-4” (1-10 cm)	2”-4” (5-10 cm)
Rhubarb	36”-48” (90-120 cm)	36”-48” (90-120 cm)
Rutabagas	6”-8” (15-20 cm)	14”-18” (35-45 cm)
Shallots	6”-8” (15-20 cm)	6”-8” (15-20 cm)
Spinach	2”-4” (5-10 cm)	12”-18” (30-45 cm)
Squash	24”-36” (60-90 cm)	60”-72” (1.5-1.8 mts)
Sweet Potatoes	12”-18” (30-45 cm)	36”-48” (90-120 cm)

Swiss Chard	6"-12" (15-30 cm)	12"-18" (30-45 cm)
Tomatoes	24"-36" (60-90 cm)	48"-60" (90-150 cm)
Turnips	2"-4" (5-10 cm)	12"-18" (30-45 cm)
Zucchini	24"-36" (60-90 cm)	36"-48" (90-120 cm)

Plant Care

Watering

Watering is essential to keep your garden alive, no matter where you live. Plants use water as a medium to transport absorbed nutrients, and it is transformed into sugar and oxygen through photosynthesis, so a lack of water is a lack of food and oxygen. Lack of water will cause drought stress in your plants, which will result in undersized fruit or no fruit at all, fibrous and bitter crops, growth stop, and wilting.

When to Water

The best way to know when it is time to water is by checking the soil. The top inch of soil can be dry, but below that depth the soil should be moist. If it isn't, you should water.

Don't wait for rain to water your garden. Dry soil can't wait. If your plants are wilting due to heat stress, don't wait for the evening or the next morning to water. Do it as soon as possible.

One Inch of Rain per Week

Vegetable gardens need one inch of rain per week but even if it has rained, you can't be sure that it's enough. Check the soil to be sure.

Many Ways to Irrigate

The more commonly used watering methods are:

- Drip, trickle, or soaker systems: This method ensures that there is low pressure and a slow flow of water by targeting the root of the plant through a system of pipes, tubes, or sprinklers, depending on the situation. While this method is more accurate, it is also more expensive and requires installation.

- Slow flow from a hose at the base of the plants: It's easy to underestimate how much water you have applied with this method. The hose should be placed near the base of the plant to target the roots, and the outflow should be reduced to avoid washing out the soil.

Remember that it's the plant roots that need the water, and that targeting the leaves can be harmful for plants. Also, sandy soils will soak up water faster than other kinds of soil.

Too Much Water

Excess water, be it from rain or from watering, can be as harmful as no water at all. It can cause rotting, reduce oxygen in the soil, produce lower quality fruit, and cause leaf diseases.

Staking

Sometimes you will need to provide some kind of support for your plants to avoid them from flopping over or falling down due to height, weight, or weather conditions. Staking can be a lifesaver in these cases, but it can also be time consuming and change the aesthetic of your garden.

Avoiding the Need for Staking

It is up to you to decide whether you want to stake your plants, but there are a few things you can do to reduce the need:

- Use a good amount of organic matter (especially in tough clay soils). This is key to proper root development and will give stability to the plant. Mulch will contribute to protecting the roots. Proper, deep watering is also important.
- Use raised beds for plants that need extra support.
- Do not over fertilize. It might give you "leggy" plants (plants with a longer stem and all the leaves at the top) which will need support.
- Give your plants the proper amount of space to grow, and they won't need to compete for nutrients and reach for the light.
- Consider wind exposure when planting. If you place your crops in a location with high-speed winds, you will need to use stakes. A better location would be against a wall or in a corner.
- Pruning can help with droopy crops and encourage strong growth.

How to stake

If your plants will not stand up without support, you might have to stake them for them to thrive. Some crop varieties of tomatoes, cucumbers, or peas will need stakes no matter what.

- Use different kinds of ties when staking: When staking a plant that will need space to grow (like a fruit tree), you can use a stretchy tie that will provide stability without restricting growth. Using twine with no stretch will give you more support.
- Place the stake to the side where it will keep the plant upright.

- Ideally you would place the stake at the time of planting to avoid damaging the root later. If this is not possible, be very careful when introducing the stake into the soil. Make sure the stake is deep enough.
- Tie the plant to the stake below the branches. A tall plant might need to be tied at several points.
- Stakes can be an eyesore, so consider using organic material that will blend with your garden like bamboo shoots, sticks, or branches.
- Some plants will need more than one stake. You can also form a tripod with three stakes for tall or heavy plants.

Pruning

Pruning, strategically cutting off leaves or branches in your garden, is sometimes needed to improve air circulation around the plant, train a plant's growth in a certain direction to improve harvest quality, or for removing dead or damaged sections. It's not always necessary, but it can be helpful depending on the circumstances.

While there are certain crops that will need pruning, there are others where it won't always be necessary. That being said, it is always a good idea to remove yellowed leaves or diseased parts of the plants.

There are different types of pruning:

- Dead Heading: This involves cutting off flower buds, usually from plants that you do not want to flower. A variation of this technique, called "crown pruning" consists of cutting the tip of a branch or stem to encourage branching.

- Pinching: This is when you remove the apical meristem, *i.e.*, the growing tips. This helps your crops to grow bushier and more compact (out instead of up), yielding more in less space.
- Thinning: This is usually done with potted plants where growth has become congested. It consists of removing some leaves and branches to allow for more air circulation and prevent diseases. Some crops will produce more when thinned out.
- Clipping: This is done to improve structure and health, to maintain a certain look in your garden, or to maximize the use of your space. Clipping can be beneficial for plants that have grown at odd angles or that will otherwise need to be trellised.

A Primer on Pruning

- To prune plants, use sharp, clean shears. With small plants you can use your fingers to pinch off damaged foliage.
- Disinfect your shears in between plants or after cutting a diseased plant to avoid the transmission of infections. Clean them with a solution of half water, half 70% isopropyl alcohol, and then rinse them with water.
- When possible, avoid cutting large branches, and don't cut more than 25% of the plant. Foliage serves a purpose, and over pruning it will be detrimental to the health of your plants.

Vegetables to Prune

- Tomatoes and Peppers: Both pruning and pinching can improve the quality of the fruit by removing competition for nutrients. The plant will yield less, but the individual vegetables will be larger.

- Cucumbers: Cucumbers need pruning to maintain a balance between fruit production and vine growth. Cucumber vines grow supported by a trellis, so any stem that is not attached to it should be pruned.
- Beans: Pruning helps with keeping bean plants upright when they are not staked or trellised.
- Asparagus: Pruning the buds at the end of the shoots is needed for asparagus to mature.
- Squash: need thinning to prevent overgrowth and any disease derived from it. Pruning helps with air circulation.

Vegetable Garden Care and Maintenance

We have talked at length about what it takes to care for and maintain a garden, but here is an itemized tip list with some basics:

- Do not be afraid of using mulch: Mulch helps with temperature regulation and water retention, it will keep weeds at bay, and it will eventually compost, adding nutrients to the soil.
- Water is key: You should regularly water your garden and check the soil humidity. Be aware of the crops that have special requirements when it comes to watering.
- Weeds are a no go: Try to stay on top of weeding your garden beds to ensure that your crops are not being robbed of the nutrients they require.
- Feeding the plants: Fertilizing will improve the quality of your crop.

- Prune when needed: Dead or diseased parts should be carefully removed to make room for new growth.
- Check on your plants: If you regularly inspect your plants, you will be able to spot pests and diseases in their early stages and treat them quickly.
- Rotate your crops: Crop rotation will prevent the soil from being depleted and will minimize the possibility of pests.
- Boost your soil: Good soil is the foundation of your garden. Keep it healthy to ensure healthy plants and a good harvest.
- Clean your tools: Dirty tools can carry diseases and pests from one plant to another, so make sure to keep them clean.
- Support your crops: Stake the plants that are heavy from fruit and growth to help avoid injuries and rot.
- Clean your garden: Dead plants, debris and waste can impact the health of your garden and attract pests.
- Harvest promptly: If you leave the produce on the plants for too long, it will start to rot, and can attract animals or pests.
- Give plants some room: Overcrowding in the garden interferes with air circulation and can cause diseases.
- Location: Choosing a good location for your garden will help you avoid many problems.
- Research your zone: You can grow any kind of plant, provided that its basic requirements are met. However, crops that thrive in your zone will

have a greater chance for success and will require less effort.

Weeds and Pests

No matter how much planning you put into it, when growing a garden, you will inevitably come across weeds and pests that can rapidly go from a nuisance to a problem.

Weeds

Weeds not only spoil the looks of your garden but also compete with your crops for nutrients, water, and light, and could potentially harbor diseases and attract insects. Here is how you can control them:

- Dig them up by the roots: This is the oldest trick in the book. It's very effective when done properly. You need to make sure to remove the entire root system to avoid regrowth. This method can be tiring if your garden is full of weeds, but you can invest in a weed pulling tool or just simply remove them by hand.
- Mulch: Weed control is one of the many benefits of mulching. The layer of mulch will suffocate the weeds and the few stragglers that survive can be hand plucked.
- Mowing: Keeping your lawn tidy will help you to control weeds by weakening them and preventing them from setting seeds. You will have to make sure to attach a basket to the lawn mower, or the clippings will spread the seeds.
- Boiling water: Scalding is a good solution for weeds that grow on paths, walkways, and

driveways, but it is not recommended for weeds that are near other plants.

- Baking soda: As a budget-friendly weed killer, you can sprinkle baking soda on top of wet weeds (to ensure that the powder will stick) or in the cracks of the pavement.
- Line your garden beds: Add a weed-proof membrane to your paths, patios and garden beds.
- Vinegar: Put it in a spray bottle and spritz it on the weeds but be very careful to avoid your crops and flowers.
- Weed burner: This works by heating the weeds to a temperature that will destroy their leaves. However, the roots will remain intact, so they will require multiple treatments or hand-pulling.
- Chemical herbicides: Use chemicals as a last resort. There are targeted formulas that can be applied to each weed and more general formulas that can be sprayed or watered into the plants. Do proper research beforehand to avoid damaging your crops.
- Proper disposal: No matter the method that you choose, proper weed disposal is essential to avoid weed seeds from spreading. You can throw them out with your general waste or burn them (though you will have to be careful, as some species can be toxic when burnt). You should never add them to your compost pile.
- Be sure to weed often and to root out the plants when they are young to keep them from spreading and gaining strength.

Keeping Critters Away

Growing delicious vegetables and fruits in your garden will surely attract animals that will regard your crops as part of their habitat. These lovely critters can be very destructive, so you will need to critter-proof your garden. Knowing which kind of animal is freeloading off your garden is essential to plan preventive measures, as not all animals will be deterred by the same obstacles.

Control Measures

- Restrict access to your garden, be it by fences, repellents or other means. Tall containers or raised beds will help keep out rabbits.
- Make your garden less attractive to critters: Eliminate holes and spaces where they could nest or hide, cover your compost pile to discourage racoons, and cultivate ornamental and aromatic plants that are known to deter wildlife. Young tender plants should be especially protected, as wild animals will favor them.

Eradication

The less agreeable solution, eradication is sometimes needed. You should be aware of zoning restrictions, local ordinances, and protected wildlife in your area. Be careful with poisons and traps, as they can pose a danger to pets.

Repellents

You can use odor or taste repellents (that are temporary and need to be reapplied) or cultivate plants that will naturally repel wild animals. Visual and auditory repellents can be effective, but over time animals will get used to them, so you will have to rotate between them.

Using human or animal hair can be a discouragement for a little while.

Pets

Though domestic animals can sometimes cause damage to your garden, they can also be a deterrent for wildlife. Cats and dogs are especially good at catching or chasing away small critters.

Live Traps

These kinds of traps allow you to catch smaller animals (usually lured by food) without harming them. The problem lies in what to do with them after they're caught. Check your area's guidelines on wildlife to be aware of prohibitions related to catching and releasing wildlife.

Fences

Fences are the most effective general measure against wildlife (except birds). Depending on your situation, you can go from chicken wire to a proper wood fence. Make sure that it's deeply buried to prevent bunnies and groundhogs from burrowing under. For bird control, you can use plastic bird netting over crops that are bearing fruit. If you live in an area with abundant wildlife, it would be best to fence the garden from the very beginning.

Pest Control

Like in the case of critters, it's impossible to completely eradicate pests from your garden. Usually, beneficial insects and pollinators will keep these pests in check, but sometimes you will have to intervene to ensure that your plants aren't damaged.

Vegetable Garden Pest Control

Integrated Pest Management

Integrated Pest Management (IPM) is the technical term for a common-sense approach to pests and their control. It's a combination of practices developed to avoid being dependent on pesticides.

IPM is a good way of keeping a balance in your garden to avoid future problems and keep the use of pesticides as a last resort. It's a good way to protect the beneficial insects and pollinators that are essential for your crops.

Prevention

The first step in preventing problems is to keep your garden healthy. Do research about your zone: which plants thrive in it, which pests are common, which crops are pest resistant. Take pests and beneficial insects into consideration when planning your garden. Once planted, water your garden regularly and keep it clean from plant debris. Rotate your crops to avoid permanent problems.

Monitoring

Inspecting your plants will help you to assess new problems: Is it an isolated issue or a developing disease? Is it an insect, an animal, or a water or nutrient deficiency? Can it spread? Is it a seasonal problem? Correct and early identification of the problem will put you on the right track to remedy it.

- Some common signs of pests: wilting, skeletonized leaves, damaged fruit, odd color changes, or webs. Remember to check the underside of your leaves.
- Nutrient issues: If you don't find signs of a pest or disease, it might be a nutrient issue. Distorted or

hook-shaped leaves, yellowing foliage, spindly or yellowed stems, extremely slow growth, purplish or blackened leaves are all signs of nutrient deficiencies.

- Signs of snacking: Munched-on leaves and foliage, pecked-at fruit and broken stems and branches might point to the presence of critters.

Analyzing

Before making any decision that could potentially harm your crops you need to analyze the costs and the benefits of the situation. Is the problem merely aesthetic? Will the repellent harm my existing crops? Will the problem go away on its own?

Control

If the problem requires you to take action, start with the gentlest solution, like hand removal, diversion crops (such as herbs or marigolds), or sticky bands. Cut infected or infested parts of plants and remove egg masses.

Sometimes pesticides will be your only option. There are a lot of organic and botanical pesticides available for use on edible crops.

Garden Pest Control Methods

Knowing your insects and their characteristics is key in applying the IPM method, and to know what measures could be taken against them.

Aphids

- What they look like: tiny, pear-shaped, with soft bodies. They can be yellow, red, black, or white. They can be winged or wingless.

- Plant damage: They form clusters in new plants and suck the sap. They don't usually kill plants, but they can cause distorted leaves and flowers.
- Garden pest control method: Knock them from the plant with a spray of water, cut the affected stem and crush them, or spray insecticidal soap. Ladybugs and lacewings keep aphids under control.

Caterpillars or Worms

- What they look like: the larval stage of moths and butterflies. In their final form they are pollinators, but as caterpillars they are damaging.
- Plant damage: They feed on leaves and stems.
- Garden pest control method: They can be left alone, unless they are causing devastating damage. They can be handpicked or left for the birds to deal with them. Row covers will prevent moths from laying eggs on the plants, but you should remove them when they begin to flower to allow for pollination.

Flea Beetles

- What they look like: tiny black or gray beetles. They hop like crickets when disturbed.
- Plant damage: They leave ragged holes on leaves, usually during spring and summer.
- Garden pest control method: Use row covers (remembering to take them off when plants flower) or sticky traps. You can plant dill, fennel, catnip, or sweet alyssum to attract parasitic wasps, its natural predator. If they become a severe infestation, you might have to use a pesticide.

Japanese Beetles

- What they look like: metallic blue or green beetles, ½ an inch long, with coppery wings.
- Plant damage: They consume leaves and flowers, leaving only the leaf veins behind. Their larvae can also cause problems in lawns by eating roots.
- Garden pest control method: Handpick them and dispose of them in soapy water. Pesticides are only helpful short-term. The best solution is planting crops they find less desirable.

Mealybugs

- What they look like: small cottony insects,
- Plant damage: They suck sap from the plants which in turn inhibits and distorts growth and leaf strength.
- Garden pest control method: Grow small-flower nectar plants to attract ladybugs, mealybug destroyers, and green lacewing larvae. Remove mealybugs with sprays of water or with alcohol-soaked cotton.

Scale Insects

- What they look like: They begin as crawlers until they find a location. Once there, they immobilize and develop a hard-oval shell.
- Plant damage: They suck vital fluids from the plants, which leads to stunted growth and yellowing.
- Garden pest control method: During the winter, you can spray woody plants with dormant oil. In spring and summer, you can spray with horticultural oil or neem.

Slugs and Snails

- What they look like: Slugs are black or brown and slimy, similar to worms but with antennae. Snails have hard circular shells.
- Plant damage: They leave holes on leaves and flowers.
- Garden pest control method: They love moisture and can be found under mulch, debris, or any moist, cool area. You can handpick them or set traps at ground level, using shallow saucers filled with beer.

Tent Caterpillars

- What they look like: the larvae of several moth species. The eggs are laid on tree branches and the larvae build silken webs as they feed on leaves.
- Plant damage: They eat leaves and can consume all the foliage of a tree if left unchecked,
- Garden pest control method: With natural predators like birds or other insects, they don't usually cause huge harm. The webs and larvae can be removed while they are small and destroyed. Some extreme cases will need pesticide.

Fire Ants

- What they look like: red ants.
- Plant damage: They feed on the stems and leaves of plants.
- Garden pest control method: Apply bait that comes in granular form and that contains an insecticide. The ants will carry the granules to the colony. You can also treat the individual mounds with liquid or granular pesticide.

Common Mistakes

Gardening is a skill that takes practice and experience. Some of its components, like weather or location, are out of the gardener's control but here are some common mistakes that you can avoid to increase your chances of success.

- Planting too early: Starting your seeds earlier than advised will result in seedlings that will have to stay in pots much longer than usual. This will stress them, and they will require more space after planting. If you decide to purchase your seedlings, don't plant them as soon as you get home. You will need to harden them and wait for the proper planting season.
- Picking a bad spot: If your garden is in an inconvenient location, you won't visit it very often, and that might cause you to overlook problems. A bad location choice might also result in poor sun exposure and improper watering.
- Skimping on soil: Soil is critical for the health of your plants. Poor soil will translate into a poor harvest. Avoid working the soil when it is soggy to avoid compactions.
- Not harvesting: Ripe vegetables that are not harvested will slow down overall plant growth. Herbs and some crops thrive when harvested often.
- Overplanting: You should not plant more than you can care for or consume. Assess the level of effort required by each crop before planting and

prioritize the plants that you consume the most or that you can't purchase locally.

- Overcrowding: Unplanted gardens can seem bare, but this does not mean that you should plant your crops too closely. Overcrowded plants will lack air circulation and will compete for nutrients.
- Not staggering your harvest: Plants that can be cultivated yearlong, or that have a longer growing season, can be planted in succession to ensure a continuous harvest. However, this method won't work with all crops and requires strategic planning beforehand.
- Neglect maintenance: Watering, fertilizing, and weeding are activities that need to be done regularly and according to the needs of every crop. When neglected, they can lead to wilting, rot, and will attract pests and diseases.
- Not fencing: Fencing from the get-go is a good way to ensure that critters will stay away from your crops.
- Ignoring small problems: Most of the issues in your garden will not require drastic actions or strong pesticides, but they will still need to be checked to assess the potential damage and plan accordingly.

Planting Vegetables in Succession

Succession planting consists of staggering the planting of your crops to have an extended harvest. You can stagger different crops or plant the same vegetable but stagger the maturity date. A well-thought-out succession gardening plan will ensure that you have fresh produce all year long.

How to Use Succession Planting in Your Garden

There are several ways to apply succession planting to your garden. The most ideal method for you will depend on your zone and your intended crops.

Same Vegetable, Staggered Planting

A lot of crops are depleted after the initial harvest. By spacing out plantings of the same vegetable every two to four weeks, you will always have a new crop coming in. The already harvested plants can be uprooted to reuse the space.

Different Vegetables in Succession

Some crops have shorter growing seasons, so instead of staggering the same vegetable, use that space for a different crop that has a later growing season. You will not have an unlimited harvest of a single crop, but there will always be fresh produce in your garden. This method works well when combining cool-season vegetables with warm-season vegetables: As the weather starts to warm up, you can start the seedlings of your spring and summer crops indoors and plant them as soon as the last frost has passed.

Paired Vegetables in the Same Spot

Each crop needs a specific set of nutrients to properly develop. Pairing two different crops in the same garden bed will prevent them from competing, as they will have different requirements.

Same Vegetables, Different Maturity Dates

Different crops have different maturity dates and growth. By planting quick growing crops with crops that will take more time you can maximize the use of your garden bed. By the time the slower growing vegetable will need more space your early season vegetable will already be harvested.

Tips for Successful Succession Planting

- Add compost or fertilizer to the soil in between each planting to maintain its fertility.
- Do not leave crops that have reached maturity hanging on the plants. Harvest them and use the space for a new crop.
- Make sure beforehand that you have enough seed for all the planned plantings.
- Cool season crops can still be planted during summer. Just make sure to cool the soil by thoroughly watering it and covering it for a few days before planting.

Designing, planning, and starting a vegetable garden is not an easy task, but it's not impossible if you put your mind to it and build a garden fitted to your needs and efforts. The more attention to detail you put in the initial stages, the fewer problems you will have later.

Once you have your garden set up, it is time to decide what crops to choose and start planting!

Chapter 2:
Edible Roots

Root crops are an extremely versatile group that can be intimidating when you first look at them. However, as we will see, they are not difficult to grow, even if they tend to take more time than other crops, and the resulting harvest can be used in a wide variety of dishes and is easy to preserve.

Beets

- Scientific name: Beta vulgaris: Amaranthaceae family
- Most common varieties: Red beets: Chioggia, Detroit Dark Red. Yellow beets: Bolder, Touchstone Gold. White beets: Avalanche, Albino.
- Best months for growing: Early spring to late summer to early fall. With the proper care, beets can be planted nearly all year long, provided that the temperatures are not higher than 75°F.
- How to plant: Soak the seeds 24 hours before planting. They can be planted on trays, but they do better if sowed directly into the soil. They can withstand low temperatures, so they will not be

affected by frost. Make sure the soil remains moist. They will need to be thinned out.

- Soil type: They can tolerate low fertility soils. Beets will not grow well in acidic soil or soil with rocks.
- Space plants: Sow seeds ½" apart, in rows 12" to 18" apart.
- Harvest: 7 to 10 weeks
- Compatible with: Onion, lettuce, cabbage, peas, strawberries
- Avoid growing close to: Spinach, Swiss chard.
- Tip: Make sure the top of the bulb is always covered by soil to avoid changes in coloring and texture.
- Culinary hints: Good for salads either fresh or boiled. Can also be pickled or used in soups.

Carrots

- Scientific name: Apiaceae: Umbelliferae family
- Most common varieties: Bolero, Danvers, Little finger, Nantes, Thumbelina
- Best months for growing: The ideal planting time is late summer into fall, because the seeds need warm temperatures to germinate but cooler temperatures to develop properly. However, you can plant them from mid-March to mid-September. They can be planted when the temperature is at least 40° F. They will not grow well at temperatures higher than 75°F.
- How to plant: It is better to plant carrots directly into the soil to avoid disturbing the roots. Try to evenly distribute the seed to avoid overcrowding.
- Soil type: Carrots thrive in deep, fertile, loose soil.

- Space plants: 1/4-inch-deep, 2 to 3 inches apart, in rows 12 to 18 inches apart
- Harvest: 12 to 18 weeks
- Compatible with: onions, rosemary, sage, leeks, lettuce, tomatoes, peas, and radishes
- Avoid growing close to: parsnips and beetroots.
- Tip: They need to be well watered to germinate properly.
- Culinary hints: can be eaten raw, roasted, or boiled, good in salads, stews, and casseroles.

Onions

- Scientific name: Amaryllidaceae: onion family Onions come in several varieties: brown, white, and red.
- Most common varieties: Yellow, Red, White, Cocktail, Cipolline. For a perennial variety, you can try Walking Egyptian onions.
- Best months for growing: It is better to plant onions in early spring, but they can be sown in any season if they are correctly cared for. The ideal temperature for planting is around 30° F.
- How to plant: Sow the seeds in trays and transplant them after four to six weeks. Choose a site with at least six hours of sunlight.
- Soil type: Onions need fertile, well-drained soil that is not compacted. They will not thrive in clay or rocky soils.
- Space plants: 4" to 6" between each bulb.
- Harvest: 3 to 4 months (some varieties can take longer).
- Compatible with: Carrots, lettuce, beets.

- Avoid growing close to: Peas and beans.
- Tip: Allow the onions to dry before storing.
- Culinary hints: can be consumed raw and pickled, they are the base of many stews.

Parsnips

- Scientific name: Apiaceae: umbelliferae family
- Most common varieties: Half-Long White, Harris Model, Hollow Crown (also known as Sugar Parsnip), Turga, All-American
- Best months for growing: They can be sown in mid-winter in trays or in the soil in early spring. Will grow at temperatures as low as 48° F.
- How to plant: Always use fresh seed and plant 1 to 2 inches deep. The seedlings will need thinning when they are 2 to 3 inches tall. Loosen the soil to at least 12" and mix in manure or compost.
- Soil type: Best grown in sandy or loamy soil, they do not do well in clay, compacted soil, or rocky soil.
- Space plants: 1" to 2" apart, in rows 18" to 24" apart.
- Harvest: 17 to 20 weeks.
- Compatible with: Peas, potatoes, radishes, garlic, Swiss chard
- Avoid growing close to: carrots.
- Tip: Parsnips are sweeter when harvested after a frost.
- Culinary hints: Peel them and roast them with other vegetables.

Potatoes

- Scientific name: Solanaceae: nightshade family
- Most common varieties: White, Red, Gold, Irish, Russet.
- Best months for growing: from January through April. The ideal planting temperature is around 45° to 55° F.
- How to plant: Use seed potatoes (potatoes from the last harvest that have shoots or eyes growing in them), cut them into pieces if they are big, and let the pieces dry for a few days before planting. Each piece should have at least one shoot. Dig a trench and plant the seeds about 5 to 8 inches deep, making sure the shoot side is up, and cover them. As the potato shoots appear, make sure to cover them with additional soil to create a mound. Keep them well watered. They can easily be grown in containers that are deep enough.
- Soil type: cold, loose, well-drained soil, with a lot of compost or manure.
- Space plants: Plant the seed potatoes 8" to 12" apart, in trenches 30" to 36" apart.
- Harvest: 15 to 20 weeks. Be careful when removing the soil to avoid damaging the tubers.
- Compatible with: Peas, beans, parsnips, turnips.
- Avoid growing close to: Cucumbers, pumpkins, sunflowers, rutabagas and tomatoes.
- Tip: Potatoes can benefit from mulch to retain moisture.
- Culinary hints: can be boiled, roasted, baked, or fried.

Radishes

- Scientific name: *Raphanus sativas: Brassicaceae* family
- Most common varieties: Cherry Belle, Champion, Spanish Black, Daikon, White Icicle.
- Best months for growing: Plant in mid-winter (4 to 6 weeks before the last frost) or early fall (4 to 6 weeks before the first frost). They don't do well in summer due to high temperatures (at 70° F or higher they will bolt).
- How to plant: Sow the radish seeds one inch deep directly into the soil and water them gently. They can be planted in succession.
- Soil type: Radishes need loose soil, rich in nutrients. They will need to be rotated to avoid depleting the soil.
- Space plants: plant the seeds 5" to 4" apart, in rows 2" to 4" apart.
- Harvest: 5 to 7 weeks.
- Compatible with: Lettuce, spinach, tomatoes.
- Avoid growing close to: Gherkins.
- Tip: Plant them in a sunny spot to prevent them from overproducing foliage rather than roots.
- Culinary hints: They can be used raw or pickled in salads and sandwiches.

Rutabagas

- Scientific name: *Brassica napus: Brassicaceae* family.
- Most common varieties: American Purple Top, Laurentian.

- Best months for growing: Plant in fall to mature over the winter. At maturing time, the temperature should not be higher than 60° to 70° F.
- How to plant: Plant the seeds ½ inch deep. When the seedlings are 3 to 4 inches high, they will need thinning. The thinned greens can be consumed. They do best in full sun but can tolerate partial shade.
- Soil type: Loamy, well drained.
- Space plants: Plant seeds 6" to 8" apart, in rows 14" to 18" apart.
- Harvest: 3 to 4 months.
- Compatible with: Peas and beans.
- Avoid growing close to: Potatoes.
- Tip: They grow well in soil where beans or peas have grown the year before.
- Culinary hints: Can be boiled or roasted.

Sweet Potatoes

- Scientific name: *Ipomoea batatas: Convolvulaceae* family.
- Most common varieties: Beauregard, Bush Porto Rico, Carolina Ruby, Centennial, Georgia Jet.
- Best months for growing: Plant the slips (small sprouts) mid-spring (3 to 4 weeks after the last frost) to grow during summer. The ideal planting temperature is around 65° F.
- How to plant: Mound up the soil about 8 inches before planting the slips. Let the plant leaves die down or turn yellow before harvesting.
- Soil type: Loose, draining soil.

- Space plants: Plant slips 12" to 18" apart, in rows 36" to 48" apart.
- Harvest: 15 to 17 weeks.
- Compatible with/Avoid growing close to: Sweet potatoes will do best in a separate bed.
- Tip: Fertilize only before planting, as fertilizing after planting will encourage vine growth.
- Culinary hints: Can be mashed, boiled, roasted, or fried.

Turnips

- Scientific name: *Brassica rapa: Brassicaceae* family.
- Most common varieties: Gold Ball, Purple Top, White Globe, Golden Globe, White Egg.
- Best months for growing: You can start turnips in trays from March to June to harvest in summer, or plant them in the soil from July to August to harvest in the fall. Ideal planting temperatures range from 40° to 75°. Can be planted in succession.
- How to plant: Sow the seeds ½ inch deep and cover with ½ inch soil. Water consistently. Depending on the spacing, they might need thinning out.
- Soil type: rich, well-drained soil.
- Space plants: Plant turnips 2" to 4" apart, in rows 12" to 18" apart. You can scatter the seeds, but later you will have to thin them out.
- Harvest: 6 to 9 weeks. You can harvest the greens when they are young by cutting them an inch from the base, as they will grow back. Do not over-

harvest the greens if you want to harvest the root as well.

- Compatible with: Peas, beans, spinach, and carrots.
- Avoid growing close to: Potatoes, tomatoes.
- Tip: Fertilize only before planting, as fertilizing after planting will encourage leaf growth.
- Culinary hints: Can be boiled, sauteed, or roasted.

Tips for growing root vegetables

- Root crops favor cool weather. They will look and taste better when planted late summer to be harvested in the fall.
- Though you can transplant most root vegetables, they will always do better when directly sown.
- The more sun, the better. Some root crops do okay in partial shade, but this can make them produce excessive foliage and smaller roots.
- Prepare your soil with enough organic matter and remove rocks and other debris to make space for correct root development. Root crops do well in raised beds. Remove weeds to avoid competition.
- Water the soil thoroughly before sowing and water consistently during the growing season.
- Spacing is important to avoid competition for the nutrients. If you notice that your seedlings are too close to each other, you will have to thin them out. Some varieties do better when crowded.

Root vegetables might not be the most intuitive crops to grow, but they have multiple uses in the kitchen and can be very rewarding to master. Remember that soil preparation and watering are key. This set of crops that will test your patience, but if you are consistent, your efforts will be compensated by a bountiful harvest

Chapter 3:
Vegetables and Fruits on the Vine

Vine vegetables have the advantage of being able to grow anywhere vertical: trellises, poles, fences, trees, other fellow crops. A great example would be to plant beans, squash and corn together. Corn will provide support for the beans and shelter for the squash. They are also harvested at the same time. This makes them ideal for gardens and households with limited space.

Beans

- Scientific name: *Phaseolus vulgaris: Fabaceae* family.
- Most common varieties: Pole Snap Beans, Fava Beans, Long Beans (also known as Asparagus Beans), Bush Snap Beans, Lima Beans, Drying Beans, Soybeans (also known as Edamame), Pinto.
- Best months for growing: Beans are best grown from April to August (you can start planting 4 to 6

weeks after the last frost). The ideal planting temperature is at least 48°F.

- How to plant: Legumes do not do well when transplanted, so you have to sow them directly in the ground. Make sure that the spot has full sun, and that other legumes have not been planted there for the last 3 rotations to avoid depleting the soil. Soak the seeds overnight before planting them, make sure to stick them into the soil with the "eye" facing down, and cover with soil, and water. If you plan to support your beans with a trellis, it's better to install it at the same time to avoid damaging the roots. Keep the soil moist during the germination, but when the seedlings are established, let the soil dry between waterings to avoid diseases.
- Soil type: Beans favor clay or silt soil, but they also need good drainage, so you will have to amend soils with excess clay.
- Space plants: For bush beans, sow the seeds 2" to 4" apart in rows 30" to 36" apart. For beans that will be trellised, sow the seeds 6" to 12" apart in rows 12" to 18" apart.
- Harvest: 9 to 11 weeks. Harvest once the pods have turned yellow-tan and are starting to crack open.
- Compatible with: Spinach, lettuce, carrots, beets, and cucumbers.
- Avoid growing close to: Garlic and onions.
- Tip: Grocery store pinto beans can be used for planting.
- Culinary hints: Can be used in salads and stews.

Cucumbers

- Scientific name: *Cucumis sativis: Cucurbitaceae* family.
- Most common varieties: For pickling cucumbers: Boston Pickling, Arkansas Little Leaf, Edmonson, Calypso. For slicing cucumbers: Ashley, Lemon, Bush Crop, Straight Eight.
- Best months for growing: Plant from March to July. For early crops you can start tray seedlings around 3 weeks before the last frost date. You can sow or transplant your cucumbers outside two weeks after the last frost date. The ideal planting temperature is 70° F. Can be planted in succession.
- How to plant: Sow the seeds one inch deep. You can also make mounds with two or three seeds each and later thin out the seedlings. After planting and watering, mulch the area to avoid weeds and diseases, and to retain moisture. If you plan to support your cucumbers with a trellis it is better to install it at the same time to avoid damaging the roots. Frequent watering is key.
- Soil type: Cucumbers need fertile soil, with good drainage.
- Space plants: For ground cucumbers, sow the seeds 8" to 10" in rows 60" apart. For trellised cucumbers, sow the seeds 2" to 3" apart in rows 30" apart.
- Harvest: 8 to 10 weeks. Regular cucumbers should be harvested when they are 6" to 8" long. Dill cucumbers should be harvested at 2" long. Do not let the cucumbers get too large or they will become bitter, and their skin will be tough.

- Compatible with: Beans, lettuce, cabbage, sunflowers.
- Avoid growing close to: Potatoes and tomatoes.
- Tip: Use a sharp knife or clippers when harvesting to avoid damaging the plant.
- Culinary hints: Can be used raw or pickled in salads and sandwiches.

Melons

Watermelon

- Scientific name: *Citrullus lanatus: Cucurbitaceae* family.
- Most common varieties: Sugar Baby, Sweet Beauty, Stone Mountain, Crimson Sweet, Jubilee II, Jamboree.
- Best months for growing: Plant in March for tray seedlings and April to May for direct sowing and transplanting seedlings. The ideal planting temperature is at least 65°F.
- How to plant: The soil needs to be warm for direct sowing and for transplants. Plant the seeds one inch deep in clusters of two or three seeds. When seedlings emerge remove the weaker plants. Harden your seedlings before transplanting them. Water regularly.
- Soil type: They need sandy loam soil with good drainage. Raised beds can help with draining and warming the soil.
- Space plants: Sow the seed clusters 18" to 24" apart, in rows 5' to 6' apart.

- Harvest: 12 to 17 weeks. The tendrils near the stem will become brown and dry when the fruit is mature, and the part of the fruit that is in contact with the ground will turn yellowish.
- Compatible with: Sweetcorn, sunflowers.
- Avoid growing close to: Potatoes.
- Tip: The more sun your plants receive, the sweeter the fruit will be.
- Culinary hints: Can be eaten in slices, in fruit salads, or juiced.

Cantaloupe and Honeydew

- Scientific name: *Cucumis melo: Cucurbitaceae* family.
- Most common varieties: Ambrosia, Edisto, Kansas, Piel de Sapo (also known as Toadskin), Top Mark.
- Best months for growing: Plant in March for tray seedlings, April to May for direct sowing and transplanting seedlings. The ideal planting temperature is above 60°F.
- How to plant: The soil needs to be warm for direct sowing and for transplants. Plant the seeds one inch deep in clusters of two or three seeds. When seedlings emerge remove the weaker plants. Harden your seedlings before transplanting them. If you plan to trellis your plants, it is better to install it at the time of planting to avoid damaging the roots. Water regularly.
- Soil type: Melons need sandy loam soil with good drainage. Raised beds can help with draining and warming the soil.

- Space plants: For floor melons, sow the seed clusters 18” to 24” apart, in rows 5’ to 6’ apart. For trellis melons, sow the seeds 12” apart.
- Harvest: 3 to 4 weeks. The tendrils near the stem will become brown and dry when the fruit is mature, and part of the netting on the surface will become coarse and rough.
- Compatible with: Peas, bush beans, onions, and carrots.
- Avoid growing close to: Pumpkin, squash, and cucumber.
- Tip: A single plant with several melons will divide the sugar between them. Thin out the fruit on the vine in succession to ripen one fruit at a time.
- Culinary hints: Can be eaten in slices, in fruit salads, or juiced.

Peas

- Scientific name: *Pisum sativum: Fabaceae* family.
- Most common varieties: Sweet Peas, Snow Peas, Snap Peas, Crowder, Pink Eyed/Purple Hull, Zipper, and Lady Peas.
- Best months for growing: Plant in March and April. Planting temperatures range from 40° to 60° F. Can be planted in succession.
- How to plant: Peas do not do well when transplanted, so they should be sown directly. Soak seeds overnight before planting and sow one inch deep. Peas should not be thinned out, and you should rotate their location every year to avoid soil depletion. If you plan to trellis your peas it is better to install it at the time of planting to avoid

damaging the roots. Water your peas sparingly unless they are wilting.

- Soil type: Peas need well-drained soil, amended with compost or manure.
- Space plants: Sow the seeds 1" to 2" apart, in rows 18" to 24" apart.
- Harvest: 2 to 3 months. Harvest snow peas when the pods are flat and have immature peas, snap peas when the pods are plump but still glossy and the pods are firm. Harvest mature pods often to keep the plants producing.
- Compatible with: Carrots, corn, cucumbers, beans.
- Avoid growing close to: Onions and garlic.
- Tip: If you prefer your peas to be less sweet, you can plant them in partial shade.
- Culinary hints: Can be eaten raw, boiled, or steamed. The pods are edible when steamed.

Peppers

- Scientific name: *Solanaceae*: nightshade family.
- Most common varieties: For sweet/bell peppers: California Wonder, Golden California Wonder, Bull Nose, Jupiter Sweet, Lady Bell, Gypsy. For hot peppers: Anaheim Chile, Ancho Poblano, Carolina Hot, Long Red Hot, Jalapeño Hot, Serano Tampiqueño, Cayenne, Habanero. For seasoning peppers: Ancho Poblano, Paprika, Aji Dulce.
- Best months for growing: Plant in late winter to early spring in seed trays, May and June for transplanting and direct sowing. The ideal planting temperature is around 65° F.

- How to plant: Sow the seeds one inch deep and water well. Keep them warm if sowing in trays. When direct sowing or transplanting, choose a spot that is sunny and bright, as peppers need warmth and sunshine to thrive. Water regularly. Most pepper varieties will need to be staked, so it is better to install them at the time of planting to avoid damaging the roots.
- Soil type: Peppers need rich soil with a continuous release fertilizer or compost mixed in.
- Space plants: Sow seeds 14" to 18" apart, in rows 18" to 24" apart.
- Harvest: 9 to 11 weeks. Harvested peppers will continue to ripen when kept indoors, so do not worry if you harvest them before full maturity.
- Compatible with/Avoid growing close to: They do better when grown in a separate bed.
- Tip: Use gloves when handling seeds and fruits of hot pepper varieties.
- Culinary hints: Can be used fresh or stir-fried. All varieties of pepper freeze very well.

Pumpkins

- Scientific name: *Cucurbita: Cucurbitaceae* family.
- Most common varieties: Cherokee Tan, Seminole, Sugar Treat, Cinderella's Carriage, Peanut, Small Sugar, Hijinks, Baby Bear.
- Best months for growing: Plant mid-winter for tray sowing, April to June for transplanting and direct sowing. Planting temperatures range from 65° to 95° F.

- How to plant: Set seeds one inch deep in hills with four or five seeds per hill. Keep moist and add mulch to retain moisture. When seedlings are 2” or 3” tall thin to two or three plants per hill. For tray sowing, harden off seedlings before transplanting. Water consistently. Pruning the vines will produce bigger fruit.
- Soil type: Pumpkins like sandy soils with high organic matter.
- Space plants: Sow seeds at 60” to 72” apart, in rows 120” to 180” apart. Unless you plan to trellis the vines, pumpkins need a lot of space.
- Harvest: 15 to 20 weeks. The skin of the pumpkin should be hard and sound hollow.
- Compatible with: Sweet corn.
- Avoid growing close to: Potatoes.
- Tip: When harvesting, leave 3 to 4 inches of the stem to increase the keeping time of the fruit.
- Culinary hints: Can be roasted or boiled.

Squash

- Scientific name: *Cucurbita pepo: Cucurbitaceae* family.
- Most common varieties are Butternut, Spaghetti, Winter, Summer Squash, and Sweet Dumpling.
- Best months for growing: For tray sowing, you can plant in early spring. For direct sowing and transplants, you can plant from April through August. The ideal planting temperature is 60° to 70° F. Can be planted in succession.
- How to plant: Sow the seeds one inch deep in clusters of two or three seeds. Water and cover

with mulch. When the seedlings have developed, they will need to be thinned. Water regularly but avoid wetting the leaves.

- Soil type: Squash needs good draining soil, with compost or a slow-release fertilizer mixed in.
- Space plants: Sow seed clusters 24” to 36” inches apart, in rows 60” to 72” apart.
- Harvest: 7 to 8 weeks. Harvest when the skin is tough.
- Compatible with: Sweet corn.
- Avoid growing close to: Melons, beets, and potatoes.
- Tip: Most varieties can be harvested and consumed young. Spaghetti squash needs to be mature to be harvested.
- Culinary hints: Can be consumed steamed, boiled, roasted, or stir-fried.

Tomatoes

- Scientific name: *Lycopersicon esculentum: Solanaceae* family.
- Most known varieties: Red, Yellow, Green, Bicolor, Purple, Black, Cherry, Currant, Pink/Pink-Red, Better Boy, Big Beef, and Celebrity.
- Best months for growing: For tray seeding you can start mid-winter. For transplants and direct sowing, from April to June. Planting temperatures range from 55° to 85° F.
- How to plant: Sow seeds ½ inch deep and keep warm. Indoor seedlings will have to be hardened off before transplanting them to garden beds. Tomatoes will need support, so it is better to install

the stakes or cages when planting to avoid damaging the roots. When transplanting seedlings, pinch off a few of the lower leaves. Water well and regularly.

- Soil type: Tomatoes need rich and well-drained soil, so they do best in sandy soil with abundant organic matter. They will do well in any type of soil, except clay soil.
- Space plants: Sow seeds or seedlings 24” to 36” apart, in rows 48” to 60” inches apart.
- Harvest: 8 to 17 weeks, depending on the variety. Leave them on the vine if possible. Harvest when they are firm and very red, no matter the size.
- Compatible with: Asparagus, basil, and garlic.
- Avoid growing close to: Potatoes and cucumbers.
- Tip: Do not refrigerate fresh garden tomatoes. This will spoil the flavor and texture. Keep them on your counter or freeze them.
- Culinary hints: Can be used fresh in salads or sandwiches, or cooked, fried, boiled, or sauced.

Zucchini

- Scientific name: *Cucurbita pepo: Cucurbitaceae* family.
- Best months for growing: Plant in March for tray sowing, April through July for direct sowing. The ideal planting temperature is around 65° to 70° F. Can be planted in succession.
- How to plant: Sow the seeds ½ inch deep. When the seedlings develop, they will need to be thinned out. Water and cover with mulch. Water consistently.

- Soil type: Zucchini likes fertile, well-drained soil, with abundant organic matter.
- Space plants: Sow seeds 24" to 36" apart, in rows 36" to 48" apart.
- Harvest: 6 to 8 weeks.
- Compatible with: Corn, beans, tomatoes.
- Avoid growing close to: Potatoes.
- Tip: Harvest often to keep the plant producing.
- Culinary hints: Can be consumed raw, roasted, or stir-fried.

Tips for growing vine vegetables and fruits

- Soil prep is key when planting vine crops. Make sure that your soil has good drainage and plenty of organic matter.
- Vine crops take up a lot of space, but if you have limited garden space, or are planting indoors, they can always be trellised.
- Vine vegetables thrive in hot weather, so don't plant them before the last frost date if possible. Most varieties aren't frost resistant.
- Water vine crops regularly but try to avoid wetting the leaves.

Vine vegetables are easy to care for and they produce bountiful harvests. Their fruit can be utilized in multiple staple dishes and are easily preserved, so they are a must for your garden.

Chapter 4: Sustainable Stalks

This particular set of crops will demand more time and effort than other crops, but the results will make it worth it. After all, there is a reason why some of them are not the easiest or cheapest to come by. But none of them are impossible to grow at home, so give it a shot!

Asparagus

- Scientific name: *Asparagus officianalis: Asparagaceae* family.
- Best months for growing: Early spring.
- How to plant:
    - To grow from seed: Soak the seeds for 24 hours before planting and sow them in trays. Keep the soil moist. When the plants reach 12 inches, harden them off for a week and plant them in a temporary garden bed after the last frost. When they mature in the fall remove the female plants (or they will be pollinated and turn into toxic berries) and plant the male plants into their definitive location. To identify male and

female plants: both produce flowers, but male asparagus have flowers with yellow or orange stamens, while female asparagus have flowers with white pistils and a green ovary.
    - To grow from crowns: The easier way of growing asparagus is to plant asparagus crowns (usually only male). Soak the crowns briefly in lukewarm water. Make a 2-inch ridge in the soil. Place the asparagus in the ridge, making sure to spread the roots out. Cover the trench with soil but be careful to not compact it. Water and add mulch. When weeding the area be careful to not disturb the roots. Water consistently.
- Soil type: Look for loose soil with good drainage. Avoid places that pool with water.
- Space plants: Plant 12" to 18" apart (from root tip to root tip), in rows 60" apart.
- Harvest: If you want your asparagus to be perennials, you should not harvest them the first two years to allow the crowns to fully establish. For established plants, harvest when they are around 8 to 10 inches high and ½ inch thick. Harvest before the spears open or the asparagus will be tough. The younger the spear, the more tender it will be.
- Compatible with: Parsley, basil, lettuce.
- Avoid growing close to: Garlic, onions, and root crops.
- Tip: Don't cut the remaining unharvested asparagus. Always leave one or two spears on the plant during the growing season. Once the foliage

dies in early winter you can cut all the spears back to ground level, fertilize and add mulch.

- Culinary hints: Can be steamed or lightly pan-fried. Never eat asparagus berries, as they are poisonous.

Corn

- Scientific name: *Zea mays, var. Rugosa: Poaceae* family.
- Most common varieties: Silver Queen, Bodacious RM, Argent, Sweet Sunshine, Golden Queen.
- Best months for growing: From March to July. The ideal planting temperature is around 60° to 65°F. Corn can be planted in succession.
- How to plant: Direct sowing is recommended. Plant two or three weeks after the last frost, when the soil is warm. Moisten the seeds, wrap them in a paper towel and store in a plastic bag for a day. Sow seeds one or two inches deep. Plant at least 10 plants together to ensure proper pollination. Water well and add mulch. When the plants are about four inches tall thin them out. Water consistently. If you are in a high wind zone, mound soil around the base of the plants to help them stand straight.
- Soil type: Corn requires well-draining soil, with compost or manure mixed in the previous fall, or aged manure mixed in before planting.
- Space plants: Sow seed 10" to 15" apart, in rows 36" to 42" apart.
- Harvest: 11 to 14 weeks, depending on the variety. When corn is mature the tassels turn brown, and

the kernels are milky. Check frequently to avoid over ripened corn.

- Compatible with: Beans, cucumber, melons, pumpkin, squash, and zucchini.
- Avoid growing close to: Celery.
- Tip: To help pollination you can shake the stalks of the plants every few days.
- Culinary hints: Can be boiled or barbecued.

Okra

- Scientific name: *Abelmoschus esculentus: Malvaceae* family.
- Most common varieties: Hill Country, Cajun Jewel, Louisiana Green Velvet, Clemson Spineless.
- Best months for growing: Plant in March for tray seeding, April to June for direct sowing. The ideal planting temperature is around 65° to 70°F.
- How to plant: Soak seeds overnight and sow one inch deep. Water and add mulch. When the seedlings are about three inches tall, they will need thinning. Water regularly. When the plants reach 5' to 6' tall you can prune the tops to encourage side branching.
- Soil type: Okra needs well-drained, fertile soil. Mix in manure or compost before planting.
- Space plants: Sow seeds 12" to 15" apart, in rows 36" to 42" apart.
- Harvest: 11 to 14 weeks. Harvest when the pods are two to four inches long. Harvest often to encourage more production.
- Compatible with: Peppers, eggplant.

- Avoid growing close to: Okra can be grown next to most plants, but it is better to avoid planting it in soil where vine crops have been planted the prior year.
- Tip: Okra has little hairs and spines that can cause irritation. Consider wearing gloves and long sleeves when handling.
- Culinary hints: Can be boiled in soups or casseroles or stir-fried.

Rhubarb

- Scientific name: *Rheum rhabarbarum: Polygonaceae* family.
- Best months for growing: Plant in late fall or early spring. Ideal growing temperatures are between 40° and 75°F.
- How to plant: Don't plant rhubarb from seed. Plant rhubarb crowns so the eyes are two inches deep with the buds facing up, and water well. Add mulch and water consistently. Rhubarb is a perennial that can produce for many years, so it should be planted in its own space.
- Soil type: Rhubarb likes fertile, well-draining soil.
- Space plants: Sow rhubarb crowns 36" to 48" apart.
- Harvest: Wait a year to harvest your rhubarb. Harvest the stalks when they are 12 to 18 inches long and ¾ inch thick by twisting them at the base or cutting them with a knife. Rhubarb leaves are toxic and non-edible, so discard them after harvesting them. Do not use them to feed animals.
- Compatible with: Cabbage, broccoli.

- Tip: If the stalks become too thin, it means that the plant's reserves are low and you should stop harvesting it.
- Culinary hints: Can be used in pies, crumbles, and jams.

Sugarcane

- Scientific name: *Saccharum officinarum: Poaceae* family.
- Best months for growing: Plant in late summer to early fall. In zones 7 and 8 it will need to be kept indoors during winter.
- How to plant: Sugarcane is almost exclusively grown from stem cuttings. You can place them on top of the soil or lightly bury them. Water well and regularly. Add mulch.
- Soil type: Use well-drained soil.
- Space plants: Space plant cuttings 6' apart.
- Harvest: 12 months. Harvest just before the first frost. Cut each stem just above the ground. Carefully remove the leaves (they can be used for mulch).
- Compatible with: Beans. Remember that sugarcane takes up a lot of space.
- Tip: When harvesting, use a sharp machete to cut the stems, and wear gloves to protect your hands from the leaves.
- Culinary hints: To extract the sugar from the cane, strip the outside of the stems and remove all the dirt. Chop into small pieces, place into a pot with water and boil for a few hours until the stems turn

brown. Strain the liquid and bring it back to a boil until it has a syrup consistency.

Sunflowers

- Scientific name: *Helianthus annuus: Asteraceae* family.
- Most common varieties: Mammoth, Teddy Bear, Autumn Beauty.
- Best months for growing: Plant in April through June. Ideal planting temperature is at least 50°F.
- How to plant: Sunflowers don't respond well to being transplanted, so it is better to sow directly into the soil or in an outdoor container. Plant the seeds one inch deep, cover with soil, and water. It is recommended to mix a light amount of fertilizer when planting to encourage strong root growth. Water regularly.
- Soil type: They like well-draining soil that is not too compacted, with compost or a slow-release fertilizer mixed in.
- Space plants: Sow seeds 6" apart, in rows 30" apart. You can plant multiple seeds and thin them out later.
- Harvest: 10 weeks. Cut the flowers about 6" below the head and let them dry until the back of the head turns brown, and the petals die down. Rub the seeded area to detach the seeds.
- Compatible with: Cucumbers, melon, corn, squash.
- Avoid growing close to: Potatoes.
- Tip: Cover the mature heads with garden fleece to avoid critters from picking the seeds.

- Culinary hints: Seeds can be consumed fresh or roasted.

Wheat

- Scientific name: *Triticum aestivum: Poaceae* family.
- Best months for growing: Plant in early fall for winter wheat, spring for spring wheat. Ideal planting temperatures are between 54° and 77°F degrees.
- How to plant: Till the soil and add the seeds. Rake the soil to work the seeds into it, water, and add mulch. Keep the soil moist.
- Soil type: Wheat needs well-draining, loamy soil.
- Harvest:4 months for spring wheat, 8 to 9 months for winter wheat. Harvest when the stalks are turning brown, and the grains are hard. Dry the stalks and shake them to release the grain.
- Compatible with: Sunflowers.
- Tip: Gather the harvested grain in a bowl and place it in front of a fan to blow the chaff from the grain.
- Culinary hints: Can be boiled or milled.

Sustainable stalk crops can seem overwhelming at first. Some of them have specific requirements, and others have growing times that seem absurd for a small-scale home garden. But once they are established, their needs are very simple and most of them will grow back each year, so don't be afraid to try your hand!

Chapter 5:
Leafy Greens

Leafy greens are not only a staple vegetable in most households, but are also a key element in a healthy, balanced diet due to their high nutritional value in vitamins, minerals, and fiber. They are easy to care for crops, with low requirements, and can be comfortably planted indoors and in containers if the weather is not benign. Let's see the main crops that you can cultivate in this category!

You will notice that this section includes crops that have already appeared in the "Roots" chapter, like turnips, beets, or sweet potatoes. While the growing information doesn't change, this chapter highlights the utility of their leaves as greens.

Arugula

- Scientific name: *Eruca versicaria: Brassicacceae* family.
- Most common varieties: Italian Rocket, Astro, Runway, Garden.

- Best months for growing: For tray seeds, they can be started as early as mid-December. For direct sowing and transplants, plant from March through July. The ideal planting temperature is at least 40°F. Arugula doesn't do well in high heat, but you can plant it in late summer or early fall for a winter harvest. Can be planted in succession.
- How to plant: Sow seeds ¼ inch deep, cover with soil, and water. Thin them when the seedlings are developed (the young leaves can be consumed). Water regularly. If temperatures are too high, provide some shade.
- Soil type: It likes well-draining soil.
- Space plants: 12" apart, in rows 10" apart. You can sow them closer together and thin them out later.
- Harvest: 4 to 7 weeks. Harvest when the leaves are around three inches long. Don't let them mature too much or they will be bitter.
- Compatible with: Beans, carrots, beets, lettuce, onion, spinach.
- Avoid growing close to: Cabbage and broccoli.
- Tip: Arugula flowers are also edible.
- Culinary hints: It is commonly used in salads, omelets, sandwiches, and pizzas.

Beets

- Scientific name: *Beta vulgaris: Amaranthaceae* family.
- Most common varieties: Red beets: Chioggia, Detroit Dark Red. Yellow beets: Bolder, Touchstone Gold. White beets: Avalanche, Albino.

- Best months for growing: Early spring to late summer to early fall. With proper care, beets can be planted nearly all year long, provided that the temperatures are not higher than 75° F.
- How to plant: Soak the seeds 24 hours before planting. They can be planted on trays, but they do better if sowed directly into the soil. They can withstand low temperatures, so they will not be affected by frost. Make sure the soil remains moist. They will need to be thinned out.
- Soil type: They can tolerate low fertility soils. Beets will not grow well in acidic soil or soil with rocks.
- Space plants: Sow seeds ½" apart, in rows 12" to 18" apart.
- Harvest: 7 to 10 weeks
- Compatible with: Onion, lettuce, cabbage, peas, strawberries.
- Avoid growing close to: Spinach, swiss chard.
- Tip: Make sure the top of the bulb is always covered by soil to avoid different coloring and texture. If you want to encourage leaf growth you can fertilize after planting.
- Culinary hints: Beet leaves can be used for salads, blanched, or cooked in stir-fries and quiches.

Broccoli

- Scientific name: *Brassica oleracea var. italica: Brassicaeae* family.
- Most common varieties: Calabrese (also known as Italian Green Sprouting), Waltham, Green Duke, Flash.

- Best months for growing: Plant January and February for tray seeding, March through April, and August through September for direct sowing and transplants. Planting temperature should be at least 40°F.
- How to plant: Sow seeds one inch deep and cover with soil. Water and add mulch. Water regularly.
- Soil type: Needs fertile, well-draining soil.
- Space plants: Sow seeds 18” to 24” apart, in rows 36” to 40” apart.
- Harvest: 10 to 16 weeks. Harvest before the buds open. If the head starts to yellow, harvest right away. It will still be edible.
- Compatible with: Cucumber, onions, rhubarb.
- Avoid growing close to: Arugula, tomatoes, peppers, eggplants.
- Tip: Broccoli is extremely sensitive to temperature extremes, so don’t plant it too early (to avoid the heads from forming too early) or in the peak of summer (to avoid early blooming).
- Culinary hints: Both the florets and the stem can be boiled, stir-fried, or roasted.

Cabbage

- Scientific name: *Brassica oleracea var. capitata: Brassicaceae* family.
- Most common varieties: Early Jersey Wakefield, Savoy Perfection, Wirosa, Gonzales, Blue Vantage, Cheers.
- Best months for growing: Plant mid-January through February for tray seeding, February

through April for direct sowing and transplants. Ideal growing temperature is 60° to 65°F.

- How to plant: Sow the seeds ½ inch deep, cover with soil, and water. Water regularly.
- Soil type: Cabbage likes well-fertilized, loamy soil.
- Space plants: 9" to 12" apart, in rows 36" to 44" apart.
- Harvest: 11 to 15 weeks. When they have reached the desired size and they are firm, cut the stem at ground level.
- Compatible with: Beets, cucumbers, onions.
- Avoid growing close to: Beans, tomatoes, peppers, eggplant, arugula.
- Tip: If you cut a ½ inch deep cross on the stump that has been left from a recently harvested cabbage, it will produce another head, though much smaller.
- Culinary hints: Can be used fresh in salads, boiled in soups and stews, pickled, or stir-fried.

Collards

- Scientific name: *Brassica oleracea var. viridis: Brassicaceae* family.
- Most common varieties: Georgia Southern, Vates, Morris Heading, Blue Max, Top Bunch, Butter Collard.
- Best months for growing: Plant from February through April, and from August through September for seed trays or direct sowing. The ideal planting temperature is between 45° and 85°F.

- How to plant: Sow seeds ½ inch deep, cover with soil, and water. Add mulch. Water regularly. Collards like full sun but can thrive in partial shade.
- Soil type: Use fertile, well-draining soil.
- Space plants: Sow 18” to 24” apart, in rows 36” to 40” apart.
- Harvest: 8 to 11 weeks. Harvest when the leaves are about 10 inches long, dark green, but still young. Older leaves may also be used. Cut each leaf, starting from the bottom and work your way up. The leaves can be harvested even if they are frozen.
- Compatible with: Beets, cucumber, onions.
- Avoid growing close to: Tomatoes, peppers, eggplant, cabbage, arugula.
- Tip: Collards are the most cold-resistant of the leafy greens, and they taste best after a frost.
- Culinary hints: Steam or stir-fry.

Kale

- Scientific name: *Brassica oleracea var. Sabellica: Brassicaceae* family.
- Most known varieties: Red Russian, Winterbor, True Siberian, Lacinato (also known as Tuscan, Black Palm Tree, or Cavil Nero).
- Best months for growing: Plant January and February for tray seeding, February through April and August for direct sowing and transplants. The ideal planting temperature is at least 40°F.
- How to plant: Sow seeds ½ inch deep, cover with soil, and water. Add mulch. Water regularly.
- Soil type: Kale prefers fertile, well-draining soil.

- Space plants: Sow 18” to 24” apart, in rows 36” to 40” apart.
- Harvest: 7 to 10 weeks. Harvest by picking the leaves starting from the bottom and working your way up. If you leave at least four leaves, the plant will keep producing new ones. When they start producing yellow flowers, it is time to completely remove the plant.
- Compatible with: Beets, cucumber, onions.
- Avoid growing close to: Tomatoes, peppers, eggplant, cabbage, arugula.
- Tip: Kale will taste better after a frost.
- Culinary hints: Can be consumed raw or steamed. The stems are usually consumed steamed or boiled.

Lettuce

- Scientific name: *Lactuca sativa: Asteraceae* family.
- Most known varieties: Butterhead, Romaine, Crisphead, Loose-Leaf, Red-leaf.
- Best months for growing: Plant January through April, and August through September. Ideal planting temperatures are between 45° and 65°F.
- How to plant: Direct sowing is recommended, though lettuce can be started in seed trays. Sow seeds ¼ inch deep (they need light to germinate, so do not plant them too deep) and water. Adjust the spacing according to the variety that you choose. Water to keep the soil moist but be careful not to overwater them. In warm temperatures lettuce can bolt (produce a central stem) and turn

bitter. You can prevent this by covering plants with a shade cloth during the warmest part of the growing season or by directly planting your lettuce crops in the shade of taller plants.
- Soil type: Use loose, well-drained soil.
- Space plants: Sow 12" inches apart. Adjust the spacing according to the variety that you choose.
- Harvest: 8 to 12 weeks. You can harvest the lettuce head and leave the stem to grow another head.
- Compatible with: Carrots, onions, beets, brassicas (cabbage, broccoli, etc)
- Avoid growing close to: Parsley and celery.
- Tip: Harvested lettuce that is wilted (but not rotten) can be revived by soaking it in cold water for 15 minutes.
- Culinary hints: Consume fresh in salads and sandwiches.

Rutabagas

- Scientific name: *Brassica napus: Brassicaceae* family.
- Most common varieties: American Purple Top, Laurentian.
- Best months for growing: Plant in fall to mature over the winter. At maturing time, the temperature should not be higher than 60° to 70°F.
- How to plant: Plant the seeds ½ inch deep. When the seedlings are 3 to 4 inches high, they will need thinning. The thinned greens can be consumed. They do best in full sun but can tolerate partial shade.
- Soil type: Loamy, well drained.

- Space plants: Plant seeds 6" to 8" apart, in rows 14" to 18" apart.
- Harvest: 3 to 4 months.
- Compatible with: Peas and beans.
- Avoid growing close to: Potatoes.
- Tip: They grow well in soil where beans or peas have grown the year before.
- Culinary hints: Young leaves can be used in salads and stir-fries, or boiled.

Sweet Potatoes

- Scientific name: *Ipomoea batatas: Convolvulaceae* family.
- Most common varieties: Beauregard, Bush Porto Rico, Carolina Ruby, Centennial, Georgia Jet.
- Best months for growing: Plant the slips (small sprouts) mid-spring (3 to 4 weeks after the last frost) to grow during summer. The ideal planting temperature is around 65° F.
- How to plant: Mound up the soil about 8 inches before planting the slips.
- Soil type: Loose, draining soil.
- Space plants: Plant slips 12" to 18" apart, in rows 36" to 48" apart.
- Harvest: 15 to 17 weeks.
- Compatible with/Avoid growing close to: Sweet potatoes will do best in a separate bed.
- Tip: If you are interested in growing sweet potatoes for their leaves, the fertilizing timing is important. As we have seen in the roots chapter, fertilizing your sweet potatoes after you have planted them will encourage a higher leaf growth.

- Culinary hints: Can be consumed boiled, steamed, or stir-fried. If you find them to be a little bitter or tough, blanch them before adding them to preparations.

Swiss Chard

- Scientific name: *Beta vulgaris subsp. Cicla: Amaranthaceae* family.
- Most common varieties: Bright Lights, Lucullus, Peppermint, Rainbow, Ruby Red.
- Best months for growing: Plant in spring or early fall. The ideal planting temperature is at least 40°F. Can be planted in succession.
- How to plant: Sow seeds one inch deep, cover with soil, and water. Add mulch to help retain moisture. Keep soil moist but not soggy.
- Soil type: Likes fertile, well-draining soil.
- Space plants: Sow seeds 6” to 12” apart, in rows 12” to 18” apart.
- Harvest: When plants are 6” to 8” tall. Cut the leaves 1” to 2” above the ground. If you regularly harvest the older leaves, the plant will continue to produce.
- Compatible with: Tomatoes, cabbages, beans, and lettuce.
- Avoid growing close to: Potatoes, corn, cucumbers or melons.
- Tip: If you want to extend the harvest, you can lift the plant with the roots and the soil around it and transfer it into a container indoors. The chard will appear limp at first, but it will rebound.

- Culinary hints: Can be used raw in salads, smoothies, sandwiches, and pizzas. Can be cooked in soups, stews, quiches, and stir-fries.

Turnips

- Scientific name: *Brassica rapa: Brassicaceae* family.
- Most common varieties: Gold Ball, Purple Top, White Globe, Golden Globe, White Egg.
- Best months for growing: You can start turnips in trays from March to June to harvest in summer, or plant them in the soil from July to August to harvest in the fall. Ideal planting temperatures range from 40° to 75°. Can be planted in succession.
- How to plant: Sow the seeds ½ inch deep and cover with ½ inch soil. Water consistently. Depending on the spacing, they might need thinning out.
- Soil type: rich, well-drained soil.
- Space plants: Plant turnips 2" to 4" apart, in rows 12" to 18" apart. You can scatter the seeds, but later you will have to thin them out.
- Harvest: 6 to 9 weeks. You can harvest the greens when they are young by cutting them an inch from the base, as they will grow back. Do not overharvest the greens if you want to harvest the root as well.
- Compatible with: Peas, beans, spinach, and carrots.
- Avoid growing close to: Potatoes, tomatoes.

- Tip: If you are interested in growing turnips for their leaves, the fertilizing timing is important. As we have seen in the roots chapter, fertilizing your turnips after you have planted them will encourage a higher leaf growth.
- Culinary hints: Turnip leaves can be consumed raw, braised, boiled, or sautéed.

Tips for Growing Leafy Greens

- Leafy greens are predominantly cool weather crops. You should keep your plants from getting too hot by watering them, using shade netting to block the sun, or simply planting them in the shade of taller crops (but make sure that they still get enough sunlight).
- Leafy greens are ideal for succession planting because they are quick growing crops that only produce a few harvests.
- Though leafy greens can be sown directly, you can use seed trays to have a steady supply of seedlings year-round.
- Leafy greens are wide crops, but their roots are not too deep. Keep this in mind when designing your garden beds or choosing your indoor containers. This also means that they need to be watered more often than other crops, but be careful to not overwater.
- Most leafy greens will grow back when cut so you can harvest again.
- High temperatures will cause your leafy greens to bolt and turn bitter.

Leafy greens are the ideal type of crop for beginners or for small or indoor gardens. You can grow, harvest, and enjoy them year-round, so they should be a staple in your home garden.

Chapter 6:
Herbs

Herbs are usually regarded as little more than something extra to add to your food and are often overlooked. That might be true but doesn't make them less of a staple for your household. They are certainly a staple in most cultures as key condiments and toppings. Most herbs are perennial, and once established they will yield produce for several years. In addition to that, they are easy to grow indoors, and even in windowsills, so you can enjoy them year-round.

Basil

- Scientific name: *Ocimum basilicum: Lamiaceae* family.
- Most common varieties: Bolloso Napoletano, Cinnamon, Lemon, Thai, Lettuce Leaf.
- Best months for growing: Plant in March for seed trays, April and May for direct sowing and transplants. Planting temperature is at least 50°F, preferably 70°F.
- How to plant: Sow seeds ¼ inch deep, cover with soil, and water. When seedlings emerge and have a

few leaves they will need to be thinned out. Water consistently.

- Soil type: Basil likes moderately fertile and well-draining soil.
- Space plants: Sow seeds 16” to 24” apart.
- Harvest: As soon as the plants are around 6” to 8” tall, you can start picking the leaves. Pick them regularly to encourage new growth.
- Compatible with: Tomatoes, peppers, any root vegetable.
- Avoid growing close to: Cucumbers.
- Tip: Basil leaves are best harvested in the morning, when they are juicier.
- Culinary hints: Can be used fresh in salads, sandwiches, or as toppings. Can be added to sauces, quiches, or used to make vinaigrettes.

Garlic

- Scientific name: *Allium sativum: Amaranthaceae* family.
- Most common varieties: Softneck, Hardneck, Turban, Elephant (has a longer growing season, so it should be planted in the fall).
- Best months for growing: Plant in fall to early winter. Some varieties can be sown in spring.
- How to plant: Garlic is usually grown from bulbs, but you will have to buy them from a garden center or a seed supplier. Supermarket bulbs will not usually work. Separate the cloves and plant them with the fat end downwards and the pointed end one inch below the surface.
- Soil type: Garlic likes fertile, well-draining soil.

- Space plants: Plant the cloves 6" apart, in rows 10" to 12" apart.
- Harvest: 17 to 25 weeks. Harvest when the leaves turn yellow. Leave the bulbs to dry for a few days.
- Compatible with: Beets, carrots, cucumbers, tomatoes, parsnips.
- Avoid growing close to: Asparagus, beans, peas, potatoes, brassicas.
- Tip: The garlic shoots, called scapes, can be consumed if harvested young.
- Culinary hints: Add to salads, stews, roasts, sauces. Can be consumed raw, roasted, or sautéed.

Mushrooms

- Scientific name: *Agaricus bisporus: Agaricaceae* family.
- Most common varieties: Portobello, Shiitake, Button, Cremini, Oyster, Porcini, Enoki.
- Best months for growing: Plant year-round for indoor growing, Spring, and early summer for outdoor planting. Most mushroom varieties are perennial.
- How to plant: Mushrooms are grown from a mushroom spawn that consists of sawdust mixed with mushroom mycelia (the root of the fungus). Your planting method will vary depending on where you grow your mushrooms.
    - Indoors: You can grow mushrooms indoors using sawdust or straw as a substrate, but you will have to sterilize it first. To do this, place the substrate in a microwave-safe container and add enough water to dampen

it. Place it in the microwave at high temperature for two minutes or until the water evaporates.

Place the substrate in a container with a large surface (foil baking trays work well for this) and add the substrate. Add the spawn using a sterilized utensil (to avoid killing or contaminating the mycelia) and place the tray onto a heating pad (the ideal temperature is 69°F), or any warm area of your house. Leave the tray somewhere dark for two or three weeks. After that time the substrate should be fully colonized and covered with white fuzz. Move it somewhere cool and dark. Remove any dark brown or green spots. To keep in moisture, cover with potting soil, dampen with water and cover with a damp towel. To help the mushrooms grow, you can add a low-heat lamp to simulate the sun. The mix should be kept cool and moist, so check regularly and mist with water when needed.

- Outdoors: Outdoor mushrooms can be grown on logs or in beds, depending on the variety.

  To grow on a log, you should start with a freshly cut log. The log should be a hardwood like maple, beech, poplar, oak, willow, or birch and about six inches in diameter and 40 inches in length. Never use old firewood. Leave the log somewhere moist for three weeks to get rid of its antifungal properties. Then, drill rows of holes one inch deep, in a diamond pattern, spacing the holes every 6 inches. Introduce the spawns into the holes with the help of a hammer and seal them using hot wax to create a seal (the wax should be as hot as possible). Make sure to label your log. Place the log somewhere shady and moist, out of the wind, but off the ground by one or two inches. Water your logs once a week.

To grow in beds, find a shady place and sprinkle the spawn between layers of substrate (you can use straw, compost, wood chips, or mixed organic matter). Keep the bed moist.

- Soil type: Indoor mushrooms will thrive in potting soil over a substrate bed, but for outdoor bed mushrooms, it's better to use substrates such as wood chips, manure, sawdust, straw, or organic matter like coffee grounds.
- Space plants: 6", if you are using a log.
- Harvest: Mushrooms are ready to be harvested as soon as the caps separate from the stems. Rinse well before consuming.
- Tip: If you are growing outdoor mushrooms, you might find that other varieties have started growing in your logs or beds. **Do not consume any variety that you have not planted.**
- Culinary hints: Mushrooms can be roasted, sautéed, stuffed and used in soups, stews, and stir-fries. Can be preserved by canning or drying.

Parsley

- Scientific name: *Petroselinum crispum: Apiaceae* family.
- Most common varieties: Italian (also known as Flat Leaf), Common (also known as curly), Japanese, Hamburg.
- Best months for growing: Plant in March for indoor tray seeding, April to July for direct sowing and transplants. The ideal planting temperature is around 70°F.
- How to plant: Soak the seeds for one or two hours before planting. Sow ¼ inch deep. Keep the soil moist. You can use mulch when planting outdoors.
- Soil type: Parsley likes well-draining soil, rich in organic matter.
- Space plants: 6" to 8" apart.
- Harvest: 7 to 9 weeks, when the leaves have 3 segments.
- Compatible with: Carrots, tomatoes, asparagus.
- Avoid growing close to: Potatoes.
- Tip: Parsley is a biennial but is commonly grown as an annual. Old plants might get tough and bitter.
- Culinary hints: Used fresh as a garnish or added to sauces.

Rosemary

- Scientific name: *Salvia rosmarinus: Lamiaceae* family.
- Best months for growing: Plant in March for indoor tray seeding, April to June for direct sowing

and transplants. The ideal growing temperature is around 70°F. Rosemary is a perennial.

- How to plant: Sow at ¼ inch deep. Rosemary needs full sun and doesn't do well in the shade. It doesn't need a lot of water so, the topsoil can dry out between waterings.
- Soil type: It needs sandy, well-drained soil.
- Space plants: 40" to 60" apart. Rosemary shrubs can get quite big, so keep that in mind when choosing the location.
- Harvest: One year. You can harvest rosemary all year long once the plant has matured.
- Compatible with: Cabbage, carrots, beans.
- Avoid growing close to: Potatoes.
- Tip: Rosemary shrubs prefer a little dryness, so avoid overwatering them.
- Culinary hints: Can be used fresh or dry to add flavor to soups, roasts, and barbecues.

Stevia

- Scientific name: *Stevia rebaudiana: Asteraceae* family.
- Best months for growing: Plant indoor tray seedlings from mid-February to March. Direct sowing and transplants from March through April. Growing temperature is at least 50°F. Stevia is a perennial.
- How to plant: Sow the seeds ½" deep, cover with soil and water. Keep the soil moist. Once the seedlings emerge, they will need to be thinned.
- Soil type: Stevia requires well-drained soil.
- Space plants: 18" apart.

- Harvest: 12 weeks. You can harvest stevia all year long once the plant has matured, but after it flowers, the leaves will lose some flavor.
- Compatible with: Basil, tomatoes.
- Avoid growing close to: Potatoes.
- Tip: Once the plant develops flowers, the leaves can get a bitter aftertaste, so pinch off the buds as they form, or prune the stem to encourage new leaves.
- Culinary hints: Use fresh or dried as a sweetener in drinks or make an extract for baking.

Herbs are easy to grow and easy to use, and they take up little to no space in your garden or your indoor containers, so they are perfect for new gardeners. Don't be afraid to give them a try!

Chapter 7:
Sweet Substitutes

The concern about sugar intake is a prevalent topic, as sugar seems to be added to every commercially produced food. If you have a sweet tooth, but want to moderate your intake, consider growing one of these substitutes.

Stevia

- Scientific name: *Stevia rebaudiana: Asteraceae* family.
- Best months for growing: Plant indoor tray seedlings from mid-February to March. Direct sowing and transplants from March through April. Growing temperature is at least 50°F. Stevia is a perennial.
- How to plant: Sow the seeds ½" deep, cover with soil and water. Keep the soil moist. Once the seedlings emerge, they will need to be thinned.
- Soil type: Stevia requires well-drained soil.
- Space plants: 18" apart.

- Harvest: 12 weeks. You can harvest stevia all year long once the plant has matured, but after it flowers, the leaves will lose some flavor.
- Compatible with: Basil, tomatoes.
- Avoid growing close to: Potatoes.
- Tip: Once the plant develops flowers, the leaves can get a bitter aftertaste, so pinch off the buds as they form, or prune the stem to encourage new leaves.
- Culinary hints: Use fresh or dried as a sweetener in drinks or make an extract for baking.

Sugar Beets

- Scientific name: *Beta vulgaris: Amaranthaceae* family.
- Most common varieties: Emblem, Owyhee, Dillon, Canyon, Oasis, Sierra, Mustang, Cassia.
- Best months for growing: Plant from March through April. Growing temperatures are around 60° to 80°F.
- How to plant: Sow the seeds 1.5 inches deep, cover with soil pressing the earth firmly on top, and water. If you want to start the seedlings indoors, do it in individual peat containers to avoid disturbing the root, and harden off the seedlings before transplanting. Each seed pod has multiple seeds, so when the seedlings each have four to six leaves thin them out. Water regularly, but don't overwater.
- Soil type: Sugar beets need well-drained soil.
- Space plants: 10" to 12" apart, in rows 18" to 24" apart.

- Harvest: 12 weeks. Loosen up the soil gently and use a garden fork to dislodge the root.
- Compatible with: Onions, lettuce, radishes, beans.
- Avoid growing close to: Potatoes.
- Tip: If you plant the seeds close the beets will be smaller, but sweeter.
- Culinary hints: Boiled sugar beets produce a syrupy liquid that can be reduced and used as a sweetener. Sugar beet leaves can be consumed as greens.

Sugarcane

- Scientific name: *Saccharum officinarum: Poaceae* family.
- Best months for growing: Plant in late summer to early fall. In zones 7 and 8 it will need to be kept indoors during winter.
- How to plant: Sugarcane is almost exclusively grown from stem cuttings. You can place them on top of the soil or lightly bury them. Water well and regularly. Add mulch.
- Soil type: Use well-drained soil.
- Space plants: Space plant cuttings 6' apart.
- Harvest: 12 months. Harvest just before the first frost. Cut each stem just above the ground. Carefully remove the leaves (they can be used for mulch).
- Compatible with: Beans. Remember that sugarcane takes up a lot of space.
- Tip: When harvesting, use a sharp machete to cut the stems, and wear gloves to protect your hands from the leaves.

- Culinary hints: To extract the sugar from the cane, strip the outside of the stems and remove all the dirt. Chop into small pieces, place into a pot with water and boil for a few hours until the stems turn brown. Strain the liquid and bring it back to a boil until it has a syrup-like consistency.

Yacon Root

- Scientific name: *Smallanthus sonchifolius: Asteraceae* family.
- Most common varieties: Red, Orange, Yellow, Pink, Purple.
- Best months for growing: Plant in April. Ideal growing temperature is from 65° to 77°F.
- How to plant: Yacon propagates by rhizomes. If your rhizomes have not sprouted, keep them somewhere dark, covered with damp sand. When they sprout, plant them one inch deep, cover with soil, and mulch them. If the plants get too tall, they might need to be staked.
- Soil type: Yacon roots need well-drained soil with added compost.
- Space plants: 30" apart, in rows 24" apart.
- Harvest: 6 to 7 months. Harvest when the plants start to brown and die. Loosen the soil carefully and extract the roots. Let the tubers dry for up to 2 weeks and store them somewhere dry and cool.
- Compatible with: Best grown in its own bed, but compatible with radish, spinach, turnip, beans, peas, and beets.
- Avoid growing close to: Potatoes.

- Tip: If you harvest the leaves early, they can be consumed in salads.
- Culinary hints: The roots can be used raw in salads or grated, juiced, and boiled to produce a syrup.

Sweet substitutes are the perfect crops so you can be more conscious of your sugar intake without having to sacrifice your love for sweets.

Chapter 8: Preserving

When talking about the preservation of food we tend to think of commercially preserved food packed with preservatives, without realizing that preserving food is a practice as old as time, one that can be easily achieved at home with a few tools. A big part of understanding the cyclical nature of gardens includes preserving seasonal crops so they can be consumed later. In this chapter, we will look at the most common preservation methods and how to properly execute them to avoid spoiling and health risks.

Canning

As a preservation method, canning is a relatively recent development. It needs to be done properly to guarantee that the food can be safely consumed afterwards.

Understanding Clostridium Botulinum

Clostridium botulinum is bacteria that causes botulism food poisoning. But it can be destroyed if processed at the correct temperatures. While usually harmless, *clostridium botulinum* can produce dangerous toxins in a moist, low-acid, oxygen free environment, or in a partial vacuum, two scenarios that can occur with preserves that have not been properly canned.

Using a boiling water bath as a way to process canned vegetables is a commonly used method, but it can't ensure that botulinum spores are eliminated.

Equipment

The safest way to can food in a way guaranteed to be safe is by pressure canning. A pressure canner is a pot that has a tight-fitting lid, an exhaust vent, a safety valve, and a pressure gauge. It should come with a metal rack to elevate the jars and prevent them from breaking. You can also use spatulas, funnels, a jar lifter, and a bubble freer to make the process easier, though they are not essential.

Filling Jars

The ideal scenario would be to can the produce a few hours after harvest, but this isn't always possible. In the meantime, place your vegetables in the refrigerator to keep them fresh. Rinse your harvest thoroughly but avoid soaking it to prevent any loss of flavor.

There are two methods to fill your jars:

- Hot pack: In this method the produce is cooked and then placed in jars with the hot liquid in which they have been cooked. The vegetables should be packed loosely because they have already shrunk during the cooking process.
- Raw pack: In this method the raw clean vegetables are packed tightly in the jar and covered with boiling water. Vegetables packed this way will shrink. Corn, beans, potatoes, and peas will

expand with this process, so they should not be packed as tightly.

Pack the jars within ½ inch of the top (one inch for starchy vegetables). With either of these two methods, salt is only for flavor and has no role as a preservative. You can add it to taste, but make sure to use canning salt.

Closing Jars

Before closing the jars, you need to remove the air bubbles that have been trapped in between the produce. To do this, insert a bubble freer or a non-metallic spatula into the jar and move along the inside walls. If needed, you can add more boiling water or cooking liquid. Wipe the rim of the jar and adjust the lid until fingertip tight. Don't close it too tight or the remaining air will have no way of escaping. Add the ring bands.

Using a Pressure Canner

To use your pressure canner, put two or three inches of hot water (or the amount indicated in the manufacturer's directions) in the canner. Place the closed jars on the rack and fasten the canner lid, leaving the vents open. Heat at the highest setting until steam flows from the vents for 10 minutes, and then put the weighted gauge on the vent pipe.

When the recommended pressure (10-pound pressure: 240°F) has been reached, and the recommended amount of time has passed, turn off the heat and remove the canner from the heat source. Allow it to cool and depressurize on its own or you could spoil the process. When the pressure reaches zero, remove the weighted gauge. Wait an additional 10 minutes before opening the lid. Be careful with the trapped steam! Remove the jars carefully (a jar lifter will come in handy here) and place them on a rack or a towel to cool untouched for 12 to 24 hours.

Checking Seals and Storing

As the jars cool you will hear a “ping” and the lids will show a small depression in the center. When they have completely cooled you can test the seal by pushing down on the center. The lid shouldn’t move. Remove the ring bands and label the jars with date, food product, and any other relevant information. Store in a cool, dark, and dry place.

Signs of Spoilage

Don’t consume food from jars that have warning signs before or after opening: leaking jars, bulging lids, jars that spurt when opened, food that looks and smells spoiled, or that has foam. Discard spoiled food and sanitize all the kitchen utensils that have been in contact with it.

Processing Time

Vegetables	Packing method	Processing time (in minutes)	
		Pints	Quarts
Asparagus	Raw or hot pack	30	40
Dry beans or peas (all varieties)	Hot pack only	75	90
Fresh beans (lima, butter, pinto, soy or shelled)	Raw or hot pack	40	50
Fresh beans (green, snap, wax, italian)	Raw or hot pack	20	25
Beets	Hot pack only	30	35
Carrots	Raw or hot pack	25	30
Corn (cream style)	Hot pack only	85	Not recommended
Corn (whole-kernel)	Raw or hot pack	55	85
Greens	How pack only	70	90
Mushrooms	Hot pack	45	Not

	only		recommended
Peas (green or English-shelled)	Raw or hot pack	40	40
Peppers	Hot pack only	35	Not recommended
White Potatoes	Hot pack only	35	40
Pumpkin or Winter Squash (cubed, never pureed or mashed)	Hot pack only	55	90
Sweet Potatoes (cubed, never pureed or mashed)	Hot pack only	65	90

Canning Tomatoes

Canning tomatoes has its own requirements due to acidity. To whole, crushed, or juiced tomatoes, add one tablespoon of bottled lemon juice or 1/4 teaspoon of citric acid per pint (or two tablespoons juice, ½ teaspoon acid per quart). You can add sugar if desired. Hot pack only.

Dehydrating

Introduction

Dried fruits and vegetables are not only easy to store and use, but the dehydration process requires less effort than other preserving methods. The compact and lightweight nature of dried produce makes it ideal for carrying around.

How Foods are Dried

Increasing the temperature of the vegetables will cause moisture evaporation. Air will then move that moisture away.

Methods

Food dehydrators are ideal for this preservation technique, though you can also use your oven: Set your oven to a temperature of 140° to 150°F and leave the oven door open two or three inches to allow moisture to escape. Convection ovens will work best as the fan will help with moving the air. Room drying is possible, provided that heat, humidity, and air movement are adequate, while sun drying is possible only in dry climates.

Procedures

- Peeling the produce is optional, though it will help with moisture release. Certain fruit and vegetable peels will toughen when dehydrated.
- Sliced pieces will dry faster than whole or halved produce, and pieces of the same size and thickness will dry evenly. Thinly slice the produce to achieve a crisp dry fruit.
- Preheat your dehydrator or oven before placing the produce to dry. After an hour reduce the temperature slightly to avoid overhardening the surface.

- Remember that dry fruit and vegetables will shrink, so use a fine mesh tray for smaller pieces.

Pretreating Fruits

Some fruits like apples, pears, and peaches will dry better if they are pretreated, which will reduce oxidation, give them better coloring, and reduce vitamin loss. They can be treated with an acidic solution, blanched, or treated with sulfite (though this last method is not recommended).

- Acidic solution: Mix a solution of 3¾ teaspoons of powdered ascorbic acid or ½ teaspoon citric acid in 2 cups of water. Submerge the cut fruit in the solution for 10 minutes before dehydrating them. If you can't get either of the acids, equal parts bottled lemon juice and water will suffice.
- Syrup blanching: Make a syrup with one cup sugar, one cup white corn syrup, and two cups water. Simmer the fruit for 10 minutes and let it sit in the hot mixture for 30 minutes. Drain, rinse, and dehydrate.
- Water blanching: Submerge the fruit in boiling water to crack the skins. This method is helpful with fruits such as blackberries or cranberries. Be careful not to boil the fruit for too long to avoid it becoming mushy. After the skin has cracked, chill quickly and dehydrate.

Conditioning and Storing Fruits

To determine whether the fruits have properly dried, press them between your fingers. They should be pliable, and no beads of moisture should appear. Place the dried fruit in an air-tight container for a few days to condition it, but if you see condensation in the container, it means it needs to be dehydrated further.

To be sure no insect eggs remain in the fruit, heat the dried fruit at 160°F for 30 minutes or chill in the freezer for 48 hours. These methods will also increase the shelf life of the dehydrated fruit.

Blanching Vegetables

You can blanche your vegetables in a solution that contains ¼ teaspoon of citric acid per quart of water, though blanching with just boiling water or steam blanching are also options. Blanching will destroy any lingering harmful microorganisms and soften the vegetable structure, making it easier to dehydrate. After blanching, submerge in cold water to stop the cooking process. Dry and dehydrate. Onions, herbs, peppers, and garlic don't need to be blanched.

Dehydrated vegetables can be used in many preparations in their dried form or by reconstituting them. To reconstitute dried leafy greens, cover with hot water and simmer until the texture is to your liking. With root or seed vegetables, soak them in cold water for an hour, then simmer to your desired tenderness.

Testing Dryness and Storage

Vegetables don't need to be conditioned like fruits do. They will be tough and crunchy when dried. Store in air-tight containers and store them in a dark place to avoid the loss of vitamins.

Leathers

Leathers are pureed fruits or vegetables that have been dried and resemble the texture of leather. Can be made of fresh, canned, or frozen fruits and vegetables. Light colored fruits might darken, so add two teaspoons of lemon juice or ⅛ teaspoon ascorbic acid for every two cups of puree to prevent this. If you wish to sweeten the puree, add ¼ to ½ cup of syrup or honey for every two cups of fruit.

Pour the puree ¼ inch thick on a tray and distribute evenly. Dehydrating puree might take longer than fresh fruit, but you will know it's done when touching the center, you see no indentation or wet spots.

Peel and roll while still warm, let cool completely and cover with plastic wrap. Leather can be kept for one month at room temperature and up to one year frozen.

Freezing

Freezing your produce is a good way to preserve taste and freshness. But to reduce the inevitable changes in texture, color, and flavor, it is important that you learn how to properly freeze, store, and thaw fruits and vegetables.

Freezing produce follows most the same basic concepts that any preserving technique:

- Choose produce that is unblemished (or clean the produce so that you are not freezing any rot). Your produce should be ripe.
- Wash and dry your produce thoroughly.
- Freeze the produce by spreading it on a single layer on a tray.

- When the produce is frozen solid, store it in air-tight containers.

How to Freeze Fruit

- For delicate fruits (like strawberries or raspberries), be sure to freeze them in a single layer. If you freeze them in a bag or container they will bruise. Once frozen solid, you can transfer them to a container.
- Fruit that tends to brown can be treated with an ascorbic acid wash (½ teaspoon ascorbic acid powder in three tablespoons water) or an acidulated water bath (one tablespoon lemon juice in one-quart water). Apply to the fruits, pat them dry and freeze.
- You can freeze fruit with a sugar syrup preparation (already described in the Dehydrating section).

How to Freeze Vegetables

- It's better to blanch vegetables before freezing them. (See the Dehydrating section for blanching instructions.) Remember to dry the produce well before freezing.
- Vegetables that hold their shape when cooked (like peas or corn) will freeze well and maintain their structure.
- Vegetables commonly used raw for salads (cabbage, celery, cucumbers, lettuce, radishes, etc.) don't freeze well, as they will become limp, retain excess water, oxidize, and change their flavor and texture. You can still blanch and freeze

them, but you will most likely have to use them in cooked preparations.

- Potatoes are better frozen raw. Baked or boiled potatoes will retain excess water and lose flavor.

Packing Produce for the Freezer

The key to storing frozen produce is to retain as much moisture as possible, while eliminating air to avoid oxidation. Pack your produce tightly and in quantities that can be used for a single meal.

Remember to label all your frozen produce with the ingredients, the date of packaging, and the amount frozen.

If you have blanched or treated your produce with syrup, cool completely before freezing and packaging.

Don't overload your freezer.

How Long Will Frozen Produce Last in the Freezer?

Frozen fruit will last for about a year, while frozen vegetables can go up to 18 months, provided all the produce has been treated (blanched, treated with a syrup, or acid wash, dried, etc.) and stored properly. The recommended freezer temperature is 0°F or lower.

Thawing Frozen Fruits and Vegetables

Frozen food needs to be thawed carefully to keep it from spoiling. While frozen produce is safe indefinitely, as soon as it begins to thaw it can potentially develop bacteria that was present prior to freezing.

The safest way to defrost food is in the fridge, but it takes longer, so you need to plan in advance: You only need to place the frozen produce in the fridge and wait for it to thaw. Depending on the volume, it might take from a few hours to a day. You can also thaw in cold water or in a microwave oven (only recommended if the food will be cooked immediately after).

Most vegetables can be boiled directly in their frozen state, though vegetables like corn do better if thawed for a bit. Fruit will thaw better at room temperature, but in a room that is not overly warm. Frozen berries will get mushy when completely defrosted, so it's better to use them partially thawed.

The water inside fruits and vegetables expands when they are frozen, causing them to get mushy when thawed. This is inevitable but can be reduced by freezing the produce at the lowest temperature possible.

Seed Saving

Saving Vegetable Seeds

Saving seeds from your harvest will allow you to plant new crops the next year, but in order to do this you have to properly choose, harvest, and store the seeds. Not all seeds are the same. You need to know the species and the characteristics of each crop in order to correctly harvest them.

Self-Pollinating Plants

Seeds from self-pollinating plants such as tomatoes, beans, or peppers require little to no treatment before they can be stored, so they are good choices to start seed-saving.

Saving seeds from biennial plants is a little bit harder, since these crops take two years to develop seeds that can be saved. Cabbage, carrots, lettuce, Swiss chard, and onions are common examples of biennial crops.

The more common self-pollinating crops are beans, broccoli, cabbage, carrots, corn, onions, and peppers.

Cross-Pollinating Plants

The issue with cross-pollinating plants is that you can never be sure that they have been pollinated by their male counterparts. In a garden with several cross-pollinating plants, a crop can be pollinated by a different variety due to the wind or a pollinator. The resulting crop will not be affected in its quality, but the seeds will grow into a plant of unknown characteristics. Plants from the Brassicaceae family (like cabbage, broccoli, or kale) and the Cucurbitaceae family (like pumpkin, squash, or zucchini) are examples of cross-pollination culprits.

If you plan to save seeds from a certain crop, but you want to make sure it's not cross-pollinating, place different varieties from the same species as far from each other as possible.

Open-Pollinating Plants

The seeds of open-pollinating plants usually resemble the original crop, even if they have been cross-pollinated by a different variety.

Hybrid Plants

Hybrid plants are the product of a cross between two varieties and combine traits of both parent plants, sometimes resulting in an exceptionally good combination that is very productive and resistant to diseases and pests. The downside of hybrids is that their seed results are impossible to predict. Also, hybrid seeds are more expensive than other types.

Harvesting

The first step to harvesting the seeds is to know at which time the seeds mature. Some crops, like cucumbers, are ready to be eaten while their seeds are still immature, so if you want to harvest seeds from these crops you will have to leave a few fruits on the plant past their harvest stage to allow for the seeds to fully mature. As a rule of thumb, crops that produce wet fruit (tomatoes, squash, cucumber) will need to be left hanging for the seeds to mature, while dry-fruit crops (grains, green leaved crops) can be collected at the same time the crop is harvested.

- Tomatoes/eggplants/crops of the squash family: Tomato seeds are the most difficult to harvest because they need to be fermented first to remove the gel-like substance they are covered with. Eggplants and crops of the squash family don't necessarily require fermentation, but they can benefit from it. To do this, after the selected fruits are ripe, cut them open and scoop out the seeds along with the liquid surrounding them. Put the seeds and the liquid with a little bit of water in a jar and cover them with a cloth to ensure aeration and to keep fruit flies away. The mixture will smell bad as it ferments, so keep it somewhere where it will not bother you. The fermentation will be complete when you see a layer of mold on top of the mixture and the seeds have sunk to the bottom. Don't let the fermentation continue past this process or the seeds will start to germinate. Remove the mold and rinse the seeds thoroughly with the help of a colander. Set them on a plate to dry for a few days.

- Other crops with wet seeds surrounded with flesh (like cucumbers or melons): Allow the selected fruits to fully ripen. Remove the pulp with the seeds and put them in water. Remove the seeds from the pulp and set them to dry for a few days.
- Peppers: Allow the selected fruits to fully ripen. When they start to wrinkle, harvest the fruit, remove the seeds, and spread them to dry.
- Dry seeds in pods or husks (beans, peas, etc.): Leave a few pods to fully dry on the plant until they start to crack open. Leave to dry for a few days before storing. Separate the seeds or store them still in the pods.

Storage

Seeds should be stored in airtight containers, in a cool, dark place. You can put the seeds in paper envelopes for easier access, but these envelopes still should be placed in a container to keep the seeds from being damaged. You can add a silica-gel desiccant to absorb moisture.

Make sure to label and date all your seeds, especially those from heirloom crops. It's better to use saved seed within one year. If stored longer, the seeds will have lower germination rates and the plants will lack vigor.

Start With Clean Seeds and Transplants

Harvesting seeds from disease-free plants is crucial to ensure that your next crops will not be contaminated or prone to disease.

If you suspect that the seeds come from a diseased plant, but you can't be sure, treat the seeds. These treatments might reduce the germination of old or poor seed, but they should not have lasting effects on good quality seed.

- Bleach treatment: Make a solution with one-part bleach to four parts water, plus a few drops of dish soap. Add the seeds, stir, and let sit for a minute. Rinse the seeds under cool running water for five minutes. Plant them directly or let them dry and store them.
- Hot water treatment: Soak seeds in hot water (100°F) for ten minutes. Transfer to water at 122°F for 25 minutes. Rinse the seeds under cool running water for five minutes. Plant them directly or let them dry and store them. This treatment can damage seeds like peas, beans, or squash, so it is not recommended.

Storing

Some fruits and vegetables can be stored fresh, and they will keep for a long time if stored properly. You should choose unblemished fruits and vegetables and check them regularly to spot any rot. They should be stored somewhere dry and well ventilated and placed in crates or shallow cardboard boxes.

- Apples and pears can be stored wrapped individually in newspaper and placed in a single layer.
- Root crops: Cut the leafy top of carrots or beets and place them in a single layer. Potatoes do well when stored in hessian or paper sacks, after you have removed all the mud and left them to dry. Parsnips

are best left in the ground and harvested as needed.

- Onions and garlic: Should be dried thoroughly and stored in a dry place. For better results hang the bulbs.
- Crops of the squash family: Can be stored for up to three months. Store them somewhere dry and well aerated. Zucchini is the exception. It needs to be kept in the fridge and will not keep for more than three weeks.
- Legumes will keep well if dried.
- Leafy crops are best used while fresh. If you want to store them, you can blanch or cook them, and then freeze them.

For other methods of storing see the Canning, Dehydrating and Freezing sections.

Rotating Crops

Crop rotation is one of the oldest agricultural practices and consists in changing the placement of your crops each year. The reasoning behind this practice is that plants of the same families have similar nutritional requirements and are susceptible to similar pests and diseases. If the plants are kept in the same area for several growing seasons, they will deplete the soil from certain nutrients and can cause the number of pests and pathogens to increase and cause sizable damage to the crops. Rotating crops allows the soil to replenish its nutrients and keeps the pests and pathogens low.

Crop rotation can be as simple or as complex as you want it to be. The best way to start is to take a look at your desired crops and identify the families they belong to.

When planning your garden, group your crops by family (for easier control of pests) and rotate their location each year.

Some points to consider when planning your rotation:

- Root crops and crops with deep roots (tomatoes, for example) will break the soil and help with aeration and water distribution, allowing the soil's nutrients to be closer to the surface. A good rotation after this crop would be a crop of a different family that has shallow roots, like leafy greens.
- Heavy vs. light feeders: You can rotate between plants that have high nutritional demands with other crops that do not require as much or cover crops that replenish the soil with nutrients.
- The minimum number of years recommended to wait before planting the same crop family in a space is three years, but you can plan longer rotations.
- Keep a record of your rotations, especially if you are planning a large garden.
- Perennial plants and herbs do not need to be moved, so keep that in mind in your rotation plan.
- If you can, include cover crops in your rotation, especially for areas where you have planted nutrition-demanding crops. You could leave these areas bare for a year and replenish with manure, but cover crops will help to keep the weeds at bay.

Month-by-Month Garden Guide

JANUARY

- Plan your upcoming garden: Research your intended crops, plan your rotations.
- Get a head start on raised beds, trellises, and cold frames.
- Wash and sterilize your equipment and your seed trays or containers.
- Start your indoor seedlings for broccoli, cabbage, lettuce, onions, and parsley.
- At the end of the month, mow your winter cover crops.

FEBRUARY

- Prune your fruit trees, berry bushes, and other woody ornamentals.
- Harden off brassica seedlings outdoors.
- Spread compost on the garden beds for the next month.
- At the end of the month, directly sow peas and parsley. If the temperature allows it, direct sow potatoes. The ideal temperature for planting is around 60-65°F.
- Turn your compost pile or start a new one.

MARCH

- Add organic matter to the soil to improve drainage.
- Start indoor seedlings of tomatoes, peppers, and eggplants.
- Test your soil if needed.
- Clean and compost any debris from the garden beds.

- If it is not too wet, start working your soil.
- By the middle of March, remove winter protection from your perennials.
- If the soil allows it, direct sow carrots, Swiss chard, peas, spinach, radishes, lettuce, onions, parsley, parsnips, and beets,
- By the end of March, harden off outdoors your onions, parsley, and any other crop that is five weeks old.

APRIL

- Add organic matter to the soil.
- Start indoor seedlings of tomatoes, eggplant, and peppers.
- Direct sow beets, turnip, carrots, spinach, Swiss chard, radish, lettuce, potatoes, parsnips, and peas.
- Remember to "hill up" and mulch your potatoes.

MAY

- Start indoor seedlings of okra, melons, pumpkin, squash, and cucumber. Remember that indoor vine crops should be started in individual peat containers to avoid disturbing the root when planting.
- Start hardening off frost-tender plants that have been started indoors.
- By the end of the month, it is safe to plant everything outdoors.
- When the soil has warmed (which depending on the year may not be until June), plant sweet potato slips.

- Keep an eye out for pests that start appearing as the weather gets warmer.
- Keep "hilling up" the potatoes.
- Start harvesting your leafy greens before they bolt.
- Make sure to have a trellis ready for your tomatoes if you have not installed one at planting time.

JUNE

- Direct sow sunflowers, basil, and other herbs.
- Continue to monitor potential pests.
- When your winter and spring crops have been harvested you can plant a summer crop. Do not keep your leafy greens in the soil much longer or they will bolt.
- Continue direct sowing warm season vegetables: beans, summer squash, and cucumbers.
- Freshen up the mulch of the plants that need it.
- Weed regularly.
- When the asparagus and rhubarb harvest has finished, remember to give them an extra fertilizer dose. As perennials, when the growing season ends, they need a dose of fertilizer to help the plants recover their strength. The plants will then stay dormant until the next growing season.

JULY

- Start indoor seedlings for fall crops.
- Direct sow kale, radish, turnips, carrots, and beets all July through August.
- Monitor your tomato leaves for possible diseases.
- Keep monitoring for pests.
- Sow a late crop of beets, summer squash, bush beans, cucumbers, carrots, summer spinach, and

Swiss chard, but cover with mulch to retain moisture.

- Water your crops regularly, preferably in the morning. Mulch to reduce evaporation.
- Harvest onions and garlic. Braid garlic tops and hang to dry. Cut onion tops and dry before storing.
- Prepare bed for fall crops. Sow a cover crop.

AUGUST

- Sow your peas in mid-August.
- Start your last indoor seedlings for fall brassica crops.
- Sow a late crop of lettuce, Swiss chard, and spinach, but make sure they are in partial shade.
- Pick summer squash and zucchini regularly to make sure the plants keep producing.
- Remove plants that have stopped producing.
- Dig your potatoes once the vines have died.
- Harvest your cantaloupe.
- If needed, sow a fall cover crop.

SEPTEMBER

- Plant spinach, collards, lettuce, kale, and arugula.
- Some pests can make a comeback this time of year, so monitor your plants.
- Start preparing for mulching your beds for the winter.
- Fall is the time to transplant and divide the perennials that should be moved every three to five years.
- Harvest pumpkins, gourds, and summer squashes that you want to store. Be sure to harvest them

before the first frost, even if they have not fully matured. They will continue to ripen after harvest.

- Harvest your second planting of radishes, broccoli, lettuce, spinach, chard, and other cold crops. For parsnips, kale, and peas it is better to wait after the first frost.
- Take advantage of fall time to improve your soil: Add manure, compost and other organic matter, and wood ashes.
- Dig up sweet potatoes while the weather is still warm.
- In late September, plant your garlic for the next year.

OCTOBER

- Plant your garlic.
- Collect soil samples for testing to fertilize for next year.
- Harvest remaining summer crops like beans, tomatoes, eggplant, and peppers before hard frost begins.
- Cut and store the remaining herbs.
- Remove asparagus tops after they turn yellow and die, but do not mulch till late winter.
- Take note of your harvest, productive and unsatisfactory crops, pests, etc.
- Cover your broccoli and cauliflower if the night is frosty.

NOVEMBER

- Keep harvesting your cabbage, kale, collards, and broccoli as long as possible. Cold frames can help you extend the season.

- For late season crops that are more sensitive to cold (like carrots, lettuce, beets, chard, rutabagas, radishes, and turnips), you can either harvest them or cover them with a thick layer of straw mulch to keep them from freezing.
- By the end of the month apply a consistent layer of protective mulch (2" to 4").
- Spread manure, rotted straw or sawdust, and leaves and plow them into the garden.
- Start digging up winter carrots.
- Plant garlic if you have not before.
- Remember to cover lettuce and other not so hardy crops during the first hard freeze.

DECEMBER

- Clean and condition your garden tools. Sharpen your hoes and spades. Clean and sharpen your pruning tools.
- Apply mulch on all your planted beds, especially those with perennials, if you have not done it already.
- Harvest kale, collards, and cabbage.
- Mulch any crop that will spend winter underground.
- Turn your compost one last time and cover it to avoid it being ruined by rain.
- Spread mulch on beds that will have spring crops.
- Review your beginning-of-year garden notes, compare results, and start planning for next year.

Preserving your harvest and planning the following year's crops finishes the cycle that you started when planning and sowing your garden. Remember that gardening is a skill that is learned by experience (your own experience and the lessons learned from others) so don't count a "failure" as such, but as an opportunity to do better in the next cycle.

Conclusion

A vegetable garden is an enterprise that can be accomplished by anyone, as long as they put their mind to it. The intent of this book is to show that careful planning is the key to a sustainable and successful garden, no matter its size or the crops grown in it.

From planning to soil prep, to choosing and growing the crops, all the way to harvesting and preserving your produce, you now have the foundation to approach the tasks at hand with confidence, and the keys to solve any problem that you might encounter along the way.

So, if you have always wanted to grow produce but you never dared, or you thought it was not for you, I hope that the knowledge contained in these pages serves as a starting point. Gardening is a rewarding hobby, and a way to be closer to nature, to have a healthier approach to food, and to take advantage of your space to grow your favorite crops.

Gardening, as we have said, is a skill that can be learned and perfected, and the cyclical nature of vegetable gardens allows you to reflect on the past cycle to do better in the next. I hope that you will start this cycle of gardening, and I wish you good luck in your planting!

If you have enjoyed this book and its contents have been helpful for you, please leave a review on Amazon!

If you'd like to be notified when my other gardening books are published, just send an email to vegetablegardeninginthesouth@gmail.com. Your information will only be used to notify you when the books are ready!

I hope you enjoy gardening as much as I!

What an engaging and fun learning experience!

Glossary

Acidic: Soil, compost, or liquid with a pH lower than 7.0 (on a scale from 0.0 to 14.0).

Aeration: Loosening the soil to allow for air circulation.

Alkaline: Soil, compost, or liquid with a pH higher than 7.0 (on a scale from 0.0 to 14.0).

Annual: A plant that blooms, produces seed, and dies in one year.

Biennial: A plant that has a cycle composed of two growing seasons. The first season it produces leaves, and the second season it produces flowers.

Blanching: Quickly scalding a vegetable in boiling water or steam

Brassicas: Plants from the *Brassicaceae* family. The best known are cabbage, broccoli, kale, rutabaga and cauliflower.

Bolting: A plant that goes to seed prematurely, usually due to exposure to heat.

Boosting (soil): To improve the structure and nutrients of the soil by adding amendments.

Clostridium Botulinum: Bacteria that causes botulism food poisoning in low-acid foods.

Coconut Coir: Fiber from the outside of the coconut husk.

Cold Frame: A covered frame to protect the crops from frost.

Companion Planting: Placing plants in a way where they help each other to grow.

Compost: Decayed organic matter rich in nutrients that is used for conditioning soil.

Cover Crop: Crops that are grown to protect the soil that otherwise would not be cultivated.

Crop Rotation: The practice of rotating the placement of your crops cyclically to avoid depleting the soil.

Cultivating: To prepare and use the soil for the growing of crops.

Cutting: Propagating a plant by using a piece of a leaf, stem, root, or bud inserted into a growing medium.

Dead Heading: Cutting off flower buds, usually from plants that you do not want to produce flowers.

Direct Sow: To plant directly into the soil.

Diversion Crops: Crops that repel pests and insects detrimental to the garden.

Fermentation: Chemical breakdown, usually manifested through effervescence and heat, caused by yeast, bacteria, and other microorganisms.

Fertilizer: Organic or synthetic material added to the soil and the plant to boost nutrients.

Frost Date: The average of the first and the last date of frost in the area.

Full Sun: 6 or more hours of unobstructed sunlight.

Fungicide: Compound used to prevent the spread of fungi.

Greensand: A marine sand rich in organic detritus that is used as a soil amendment.

Green Manure: Crops planted with the purpose of being incorporated into the soil while they are still green, to serve as added nutrients.

Hardening Off: Acclimatizing indoor plants to outdoor conditions.

Hardiness: Capacity of a plant to tolerate the cold.

Hardiness Zones: System used by the USDA that divides the United States territory in zones by their minimum average annual temperature.

Harvesting: The act of collecting mature crop produce.

Heat Zones: System used by the American Horticultural Society that divides the United States territory in zones by their maximum average annual temperature.

Humus: Substance created from the decomposition of organic material such as clippings, dead plants, and leaves.

Integrated Pest Management (IPM): A pest control strategy that combines several methods (natural predators and parasites, physical techniques, cultural practices, biological controls, and pesticides).

Legumes: Family of plants characterized by having their seeds in a pod.

Loam: Fertile soil with a balanced amount of clay, sand, and humus.

Manure: animal feces (usually mixed with straw and other litter) used as a soil amendment.

Mulch: Organic material (like straw, grass, or wood chips) that is spread on the soil to help with heat and water retention.

Mulching: The act of applying mulch to the soil or crops.

Mycorrhizae: Fungus that grows in a parasitic relationship with the roots of a plant.

N-P-K: Abbreviation of Nitrogen-Phosphorus-Potassium, the three main nutrients that crops need to thrive.

Nutrients: Substances that provide the necessary nourishment for the plants.

Organic: Derived from living organisms and made up from carbon-based compounds.

Overcrowding: Growing crops extremely close to each other.

Oxidation: Chemical reaction that occurs when certain substances come in contact with oxygen. known for causing a dark color in uncooked fruits and vegetables.

Partial Sun/Partial Shade: Less than 6 hours of unobstructed sunlight.

Peat Containers: Biodegradable containers that can be planted with the seedling and that will disintegrate and mix into the soil.

Perennial: A plant that grows and flowers for years.

Pest: Destructive insect or animal that attacks and destroys crops.

pH: A scale from 0.0 to 14.0, with 7.0 being neutral, that describes the acidity or alkalinity of a soil, compost or liquid.

Pinching: Removal of growing tips to encourage new branches.

Pollinating: The act of transporting pollen from one part of the plant to another to ensure the production of seeds.

Preserving: Treating food to prevent it from rotting.

Pruning: To trim parts of a plant to encourage growth.

Rhizome: The underground stem of certain plants that can produce new shoots and roots.

Root: Underground section of a plant that absorbs and stores water, oxygen, and nutrients.

Seed Tray: A tray used to plant multiple seedlings at the time.

Seedling: A young plant grown from a seed.

Silt: Loose sedimentary material found in soil.

Soil amendment: Material added to the soil to improve its properties.

Soil test: A test to measure the nutrients and pH of your soil.

Sow: The act of planting a seed.

Staking: Using a stake to support a plant.

Sticky Bands: Pest control device that consists of a band covered by a sticky substance that traps any insect that comes in contact with it.

Substrate: Base on which lives an organism, and from where it receives nourishment.

Succession Planting: Staggering the planting of your crops to have an extended harvest.

Thinning Out: Removing some leaves and branches to allow for more air circulation and prevent diseases.

Till: To turn over the topsoil as a preparation for planting.

Topsoil: The top layer of soil.

Transpiration: Loss of water vapor in the plants.

Transplanting: Moving a plant from one medium to another.

Trellis: A structure that supports plants that are tall, floppy, or that grow on a vine.

Tropical (climate): A climate that is warm all year round.

Tropical (plant): A plant that is native to a tropical climate.

Vermicomposting: The use of worms to convert organic waste into compost.

Weeding: The act of removing weeds from your garden.

Wood Ash: Residue that remains after the combustion of wood.

References

12 Benefits of Having a Vegetable Garden. (2021, March 19). Gaias Organic Gardens. https://www.gaiasorganicgardens.com.au/12-benefits-vegetable-garden

15 Surprising Vegetable Garden Statistics (2021) | Home Garden. (n.d.). Cooped up Life. https://coopeduplife.com/vegetable-garden-statistics/

Allen Smith, P. (2017, October 2). *Growing and Harvesting Spaghetti Squash*. P. Allen Smith. https://pallensmith.com/2017/10/02/growing-harvesting-spaghetti-squash/

Amy Grant. (2021, July 27). *Can I Grow Wheat At Home: Tips For Growing Wheat In Home Gardens* Www.gardeningknowhow.com. https://www.gardeningknowhow.com/edible/grains/wheat/growing-wheat-in-home-gardens.htm

Arugula Zone Planting Guide. (n.d.). Www.miraclegro.com. Retrieved December 6, 2022, from https://www.miraclegro.com/en-us/arugula-zone-planting-guide

Baessler, L. (n.d.). *Yacon Root Info - How To Grow Yacon Plants In The Garden*. Gardening Know How. Retrieved December 6, 2022, from https://www.gardeningknowhow.com/edible/herbs/yacon/yacon-plant-care.htm

Ballew, J. (2021, November 4). *Managing Fire Ants in the Vegetable Garden*. Home & Garden Information Center | Clemson University, South Carolina.

https://hgic.clemson.edu/factsheet/controlling-fire-ants-in-the-vegetable-garden/

Barton, R. (n.d.). *Know Your Garden Soil: How to Make the Most of Your Soil Type*. Eartheasy Guides & Articles. Retrieved December 6, 2022, from https://learn.eartheasy.com/articles/know-your-garden-soil-how-to-make-the-most-of-your-soil-type

BBC Gardeners' World Magazine. (2020, April 6). *How to grow butternut squash*. BBC Gardeners World Magazine. https://www.gardenersworld.com/how-to/grow-plants/how-to-grow-butternut-squash

Beytes, C. (n.d.). *A College Class Asks: Why Don't People Garden?* Www.growertalks.com. https://www.growertalks.com/Article/?articleid=20101

Bradbury, K. (2010, November 5). *Storing and Preserving Your Garden Harvest*. GrowVeg. https://www.growveg.com/guides/storing-and-preserving-your-garden-harvest/

Brandenberger, L., Dunn, B., & Shrefler, J. (2017, February 1). *Growing Vegetable Transplants* - Oklahoma State University. Extension.okstate.edu. https://extension.okstate.edu/fact-sheets/growing-vegetable-transplants.html

Broccoli Zone Planting Guide. (n.d.). Www.miraclegro.com. Retrieved December 6, 2022, from https://www.miraclegro.com/en-us/broccoli-zone-planting-guide

Butler, J. (2022, April 26). *How to Plant and Grow Pinto Beans* | Gardener's Path. Gardener's Path. https://gardenerspath.com/plants/vegetables/grow-pinto-beans/

Cabbage Zone Planting Guide. (n.d.). Www.miraclegro.com. Retrieved December 6, 2022, from https://www.miraclegro.com/en-us/cabbage-zone-planting-guide

Caroly. (2017, June 15). *Growing Mushrooms : How To Grow Mushrooms Indoors*. Gardenoid. https://www.gardenoid.com/how-to-grow-mushrooms-indoors/

Cowpea: Pinkeye Purple Hull. (n.d.). Www.smartgardener.com. Retrieved December 6, 2022, from https://www.smartgardener.com/plants/1705-cowpea-pinkeye-purple-hull/overview

Crossley, H., Wilson, S., & Reaney, H. (2021, June 4). *How to get rid of weeds and stop them from spreading: remove these pesky plants from your garden borders*. Gardeningetc.com. https://www.gardeningetc.com/advice/how-to-get-rid-of-weeds-and-stop-them-from-spreading

Ellis, M. E. (n.d.). *USDA Zone Explanation – What Do Hardiness Zones Mean Exactly*. Www.gardeningknowhow.com. Retrieved December 6, 2022, from https://www.gardeningknowhow.com/planting-zones/what-do-hardiness-zones-mean.htm

Food Preservation: Basics for Canning Vegetables. (2015, May 28). Ohioline.osu.edu. https://ohioline.osu.edu/factsheet/HYG-5344

Garcia, R. (2020, September 29). *How to Grow Sugar Cane For A Sweet Treat*. Epic Gardening. https://www.epicgardening.com/how-to-grow-sugar-cane/

Garden-Robinson, J. (2017, November 26). *Food Preservation: Drying Vegetables.* NDSU Agriculture and Extension. https://www.ndsu.edu/agriculture/extension/publications/food-preservation-drying-vegetables

Gardenate - *Growing Asparagus*. (n.d.). Gardenate.com. Retrieved December 6, 2022, from https://www.gardenate.com/plant/Asparagus

Gardenate - *Growing Basil.* (n.d.). Gardenate.com. Retrieved December 6, 2022, from https://www.gardenate.com/plant/Basil

Gardenate - *Growing Beans - climbing*. (n.d.). Gardenate.com. Retrieved December 6, 2022, from https://www.gardenate.com/plant/Beans%2B-%2Bclimbing

Gardenate - *Growing Beetroot. (n.d.).* Gardenate.com. Retrieved December 6, 2022, from https://www.gardenate.com/plant/Beetroot

Gardenate - *Growing Broccoli. (n.d.).* Gardenate.com. Retrieved December 6, 2022, from https://www.gardenate.com/plant/Broccoli

Gardenate - *Growing Cabbage*. (n.d.). Gardenate.com. Retrieved December 6, 2022, from https://www.gardenate.com/plant/Cabbage

Gardenate - *Growing Carrot.* (n.d.). Gardenate.com. Retrieved December 6, 2022, from https://www.gardenate.com/plant/Carrot

Gardenate - *Growing Chilli peppers.* (n.d.). Gardenate.com. Retrieved December 6, 2022, from https://www.gardenate.com/plant/Chilli%2Bpeppers

Gardenate - *Growing Cucumber*. (n.d.). Gardenate.com. https://www.gardenate.com/plant/Cucumber

Gardenate - *Growing Garlic*. (n.d.). Gardenate.com. Retrieved December 6, 2022, from https://www.gardenate.com/plant/Garlic

Gardenate - *Growing Kale*. (n.d.). Gardenate.com. Retrieved December 6, 2022, from https://www.gardenate.com/plant/Kale

Gardenate - *Growing Lettuce*. (n.d.). Gardenate.com. Retrieved December 6, 2022, from https://www.gardenate.com/plant/Lettuce

Gardenate - *Growing Okra*. (n.d.). Gardenate.com. Retrieved December 6, 2022, from https://www.gardenate.com/plant/Okra

Gardenate - *Growing Onion*. (n.d.). Gardenate.com. Retrieved December 6, 2022, from https://www.gardenate.com/plant/Onion

Gardenate - *Growing Parsley*. (n.d.). Gardenate.com. Retrieved December 6, 2022, from https://www.gardenate.com/plant/Parsley

Gardenate - *Growing Parsnip*. (n.d.). Gardenate.com. Retrieved December 6, 2022, from https://www.gardenate.com/plant/Parsnip

Gardenate - *Growing Peas*. (n.d.). Gardenate.com. https://www.gardenate.com/plant/Peas

Gardenate - *Growing Potato*. (n.d.). Gardenate.com. Retrieved December 6, 2022, from https://www.gardenate.com/plant/Potato

Gardenate - *Growing Pumpkin*. (n.d.). Gardenate.com. Retrieved December 6, 2022, from https://www.gardenate.com/plant/Pumpkin

Gardenate - *Growing Radish*. (n.d.). Gardenate.com. Retrieved December 6, 2022, from https://www.gardenate.com/plant/Radish

Gardenate - *Growing Rhubarb*. (n.d.). Gardenate.com. Retrieved December 6, 2022, from https://www.gardenate.com/plant/Rhubarb

Gardenate - *Growing Rosemary*. (n.d.). Gardenate.com. Retrieved December 6, 2022, from https://www.gardenate.com/plant/Rosemary

Gardenate - *Growing Rutabaga*. (n.d.). Gardenate.com. Retrieved December 6, 2022, from https://www.gardenate.com/plant/Rutabaga

Gardenate - *Growing Squash*. (n.d.). Gardenate.com. Retrieved December 6, 2022, from https://www.gardenate.com/plant/Squash

Gardenate - *Growing Sunflower*. (n.d.). Gardenate.com. Retrieved December 6, 2022, from https://www.gardenate.com/plant/Sunflower

Gardenate - *Growing Sweet corn*. (n.d.). Gardenate.com. Retrieved December 6, 2022, from https://www.gardenate.com/plant/Sweet%2Bcorn

Gardenate - *Growing Sweet Potato*. (n.d.). Gardenate.com. Retrieved December 6, 2022, from https://www.gardenate.com/plant/Sweet%2BPotato

Gardenate - *Growing Tomato*. (n.d.). Gardenate.com. Retrieved December 6, 2022, from https://www.gardenate.com/plant/Tomato

Gardenate - *Growing Turnip*. (n.d.). Gardenate.com. Retrieved December 6, 2022, from https://www.gardenate.com/plant/Turnip

Gardenate - *Growing Watermelon*. (n.d.). Gardenate.com. Retrieved December 6, 2022, from https://www.gardenate.com/plant/Watermelon

Gardenate - *Growing Yacon*. (n.d.). Gardenate.com. Retrieved December 6, 2022, from https://www.gardenate.com/plant/Yacon

Gardenate - *Growing Zucchini*. (n.d.). Gardenate.com. Retrieved December 6, 2022, from https://www.gardenate.com/plant/Zucchini

Gardeners' World Magazine. (2022, February 16). *How to grow elephant garlic*. BBC Gardeners World Magazine. https://www.gardenersworld.com/how-to/grow-plants/how-to-grow-elephant-garlic/

Gibson, M. (2019, March 4). *Staking Your Garden Plants: When, Why, and How*. Gardening Channel. https://www.gardeningchannel.com/staking-your-garden-plants-guide/

Grant, A. (n.d.). *Vegetable Garden Fertilizers – Types Of Fertilizer For Vegetable Gardens*. Gardening Know How. Retrieved December 6, 2022, from https://www.gardeningknowhow.com/edible/vegetables/vgen/fertilizer-options-for-your-vegetable-garden.htm

Grant, A. (2021a, April 16). *Purple Hull Pea Maintenance: Tips On Growing Purple Hull Peas*. Gardening Know How. https://www.gardeningknowhow.com/edible/vegetables/beans/how-to-grow-purple-hull-peas.htm

Grant, A. (2021b, November 14). *Sweet Dumpling Squash Plants: Growing Sweet Dumpling Squash In The Garden*. Gardening Know How. https://www.gardeningknowhow.com/edible/vegetables/squash/sweet-dumpling-acorn-squash.htm

Growing Carrots Year-Round: A Strategy for Success. (2013, October 10). Tenth Acre Farm. https://www.tenthacrefarm.com/growing-carrots-year-round/

Growing Peppers | Planting & General Growing Tips. (n.d.). Bonnie Plants. Retrieved December 6, 2022, from https://bonnieplants.com/blogs/how-to-grow/growing-peppers

Growing Squash Plants | General Planting & Growing Tips. (n.d.). Bonnie Plants. Retrieved December 6, 2022, from https://bonnieplants.com/blogs/how-to-grow/growing-squash

How and When to Fertilize Your Vegetable Garden. (2022, May 27). Almanac. https://www.almanac.com/how-fertilize-your-vegetable-garden

How to Freeze Fruits and Vegetables to Preserve Freshness. (2021, March 4). Allrecipes. https://www.allrecipes.com/article/how-to-freeze-fruits-and-vegetables/

How to Grow Cantaloupe & Honeydew Melons. (n.d.). Bonnie Plants. Retrieved December 6, 2022, from https://bonnieplants.com/blogs/how-to-grow/growing-cantaloupe-and-honeydew-melons

How to Grow Collard Greens | Learn More About the Collard Plant. (n.d.). Bonnie Plants. Retrieved

December 6, 2022, from
https://bonnieplants.com/blogs/how-to-grow/growing-collards

How to Grow Stevia From Seeds and Cuttings. (2022, June 7). MasterClass.
https://www.masterclass.com/articles/how-to-grow-stevia-from-seeds-and-cuttings

How to Grow Sugar Cane: Caring for Sugar Cane Plants. (2021, August 13). MasterClass.
https://www.masterclass.com/articles/how-to-grow-sugar-cane

How to Grow Veg from Seed - Garden Advice - Westland Garden Health. (n.d.). Garden Health. Retrieved December 6, 2022, from
https://www.gardenhealth.com/advice/grow-your-own/how-to-grow-veg-from-seed

How to Grow Wheat – A Step-by-Step Guide | Nestlé Cereals. (n.d.). Www.nestle-Cereals.com. Retrieved December 6, 2022, from https://www.nestle-cereals.com/uk/blog/kids-activities/how-to-grow-grain

How to Lay Out a Vegetable Garden. (2022, February 25). Almanac.com.
https://www.almanac.com/video/how-lay-out-vegetable-garden

How to Plant & Grow Zucchini. (n.d.). Www.miraclegro.com. Retrieved December 6, 2022, from https://www.miraclegro.com/en-us/library/edible-gardening/how-plant-grow-zucchini

How to Plant and Grow Kale | General Planting & Growing Tips. (n.d.). Bonnie Plants. Retrieved December 6, 2022, from https://bonnieplants.com/blogs/how-to-grow/growing-kale

How to Save Seeds - Seed Savers Exchange. (n.d.). Www.seedsavers.org. Retrieved December 6, 2022, from https://www.seedsavers.org/how-to-save-seeds

Hu, S. (2020, July 20). *Composting 101.* NRDC. https://www.nrdc.org/stories/composting-101

Ianotti, M. (2021a, February 28). *Controlling Insect and Diseases in the Vegetable Garden.* The Spruce. https://www.thespruce.com/garden-pest-control-1402737

Ianotti, M. (2021b, July 27). *What Is Succession Planting?* The Spruce. https://www.thespruce.com/succession-planting-1403366

Ianotti, M. (2021c, August 3). *How to Design Your Ideal Vegetable Garden.* The Spruce. https://www.thespruce.com/designing-vegetable-gardens-1403407

Ianotti, M. (2022a, February 9). *10 Biggest Vegetable Gardening Mistakes We've All Made.* The Spruce. https://www.thespruce.com/biggest-vegetable-gardening-mistakes-1402993

Ianotti, M. (2022b, April 20). *How to Grow Rutabaga, the Turnip's Quirky Cousin*. The Spruce. https://www.thespruce.com/how-to-grow-rutabaga-1403471

Ianotti, M. (2022c, April 20). *How to Grow Swiss Chard.* The Spruce.

https://www.thespruce.com/growing-swiss-chard-1403466

Ianotti, M. (2022d, April 27). *You Can Have a Vegetable Garden Even if You Don't Have Much Space.* The Spruce. https://www.thespruce.com/vegetable-gardening-in-small-spaces-1403451

Ianotti, M. (2022e, July 31). *How to Grow Rosemary Indoors and Out*. The Spruce. https://www.thespruce.com/grow-and-care-for-rosemary-plants-1403406

Kale Zone Planting Guide. (n.d.). Www.miraclegro.com. Retrieved December 6, 2022, from https://www.miraclegro.com/en-us/kale-zone-planting-guide

LaBorde, L., Zepp, M., & Hirneisen, A. (2019, March 13). *Let's Preserve: Drying Fruits and Vegetables (Dehydration).* Penn State Extension. https://extension.psu.edu/lets-preserve-drying-fruits-and-vegetables-dehydration

LaLiberte, K. (2022, November 22). *Keeping Animal Pests Out of Your Garden* | Gardener's Supply. Gardeners Supply. https://www.gardeners.com/how-to/keep-animals-out-of-your-garden/5426.html

Lavezzo, A. (n.d.). Zone 7 - *Monthly Garden Calendar: Chores and Planting Guide.* Sow True Seed. Retrieved December 6, 2022, from https://sowtrueseed.com/blogs/monthly-garden-schedule-by-zone/zone-7-monthly-garden-calendar-chores-and-planting-guide

Lenhof, R. (2021, July 15). *Pruning Vegetables: What Plants to Prune and Which Ones Not To.* House Fur.

https://housefur.com/pruning-vegetables-what-plants-to-prune-and-which-ones-not-to/

Lofgren, K. (2021, August 16). *How to Grow Sugar Beets* | Gardener's Path. Gardener's Path. https://gardenerspath.com/plants/vegetables/grow-sugar-beets/

MacKenzie, J. (2018). *Watering the vegetable garden.* Extension.umn.edu. https://extension.umn.edu/water-wisely-start-your-own-backyard/watering-vegetable-garden

MacKenzie, J., & Grabowski, M. (2018). *Saving vegetable seeds.* Extension.umn.edu. https://extension.umn.edu/planting-and-growing-guides/saving-vegetable-seeds

Marsden, C. (2012, April 9). *Using Crop Rotation in a Home Vegetable Garden.* Wisconsin Horticulture. https://hort.extension.wisc.edu/articles/using-crop-rotation-home-vegetable-garden-0/

Michaels, K. (2022, April 20). *How to Grow Arugula in a Container or Herb Garden.* The Spruce. https://www.thespruce.com/growing-arugula-in-garden-pots-848160

National Center for Home Food Preservation | *How Do I? Can Fruits.* (n.d.). Nchfp.uga.edu. Retrieved December 6, 2022, from https://nchfp.uga.edu/how/gen_freeze.html#gsc.tab=0

NOAA's National Weather Service Climate Services Program. (n.d.). *How do I utilize the Weather and Climate information for successful gardening?* NOAA's National Weather Service. Retrieved December 6, 2022, from https://www.weather.gov/media/dvn/Brochures/Weather_Gardening.pdf

Old Farmer's Almanac. (n.d.-a). *Crop Rotation 101: Tips for Vegetable Gardens*. Almanac.com. Retrieved December 6, 2022, from https://www.almanac.com/crop-rotation-101-tips-vegetable-gardens

Old Farmer's Almanac. (n.d.-b). *First and Last Frost Dates by ZIP Code* | The Old Farmer's Almanac. Almanac.com. Retrieved December 6, 2022, from https://www.almanac.com/gardening/frostdates

Old Farmer's Almanac. (n.d.). *Pumpkins*. Old Farmer's Almanac. Retrieved December 6, 2022, from https://www.almanac.com/plant/pumpkins

Old Farmer's Almanac. (2018, November 7). *Parsnips*. Old Farmer's Almanac. https://www.almanac.com/plant/parsnips

Old Farmer's Almanac. (2019a, March 26). *Peas*. Old Farmer's Almanac. https://www.almanac.com/plant/peas

Old Farmer's Almanac. (2019b, March 27). *Sunflowers*. Old Farmer's Almanac. https://www.almanac.com/plant/sunflowers

Old Farmer's Almanac. (2019c, April 4). *Lettuce*. Old Farmer's Almanac. https://www.almanac.com/plant/lettuce

Old Farmer's Almanac. (2019d, May 19). *Tomatoes*. Old Farmer's Almanac. https://www.almanac.com/plant/tomatoes

Old Farmer's Almanac. (2019e, June 11). *Cucumbers*. Old Farmer's Almanac. https://www.almanac.com/plant/cucumbers

Old Farmer's Almanac. (2019e, June 28). *Beets*. Old Farmer's Almanac. https://www.almanac.com/plant/beets

Old Farmer's Almanac. (2019f, July). *Arugula*. Old Farmer's Almanac. https://www.almanac.com/plant/arugula

Old Farmer's Almanac. (2019g, July 5). *Corn*. Old Farmer's Almanac. https://www.almanac.com/plant/corn

Old Farmer's Almanac. (2019h, July 25). *Asparagus*. Old Farmer's Almanac. https://www.almanac.com/plant/asparagus

Old Farmer's Almanac. (2019i, July 28). Parsley. Old Farmer's Almanac. https://www.almanac.com/plant/parsley

Old Farmer's Almanac. (2019j, September 2). *Basil*. Old Farmer's Almanac. https://www.almanac.com/plant/basil

Old Farmer's Almanac. (2019k, October 5). *Okra*. Old Farmer's Almanac. https://www.almanac.com/plant/okra

Old Farmer's Almanac. (2019l, October 23). *Rhubarb*. Old Farmer's Almanac. https://www.almanac.com/plant/rhubarb

Old Farmer's Almanac. (2022a, May 27). *How and When to Fertilize Your Vegetable Garden*. Old Farmer's

Almanac. https://www.almanac.com/how-fertilize-your-vegetable-garden

Old Farmer's Almanac. (2022b, October 14). *Soil Preparation: How Do You Prepare Garden Soil for Planting?* Almanac.com. https://www.almanac.com/soil-preparation-how-do-you-prepare-garden-soil-planting

Planting and Growing Onions In Zone 7. (2022, March 30). GFL Outdoors. https://www.gfloutdoors.com/planting-and-growing-onions-in-zone-7/

Planting and Harvesting Mushrooms Timelines. (n.d.). Www.fieldforest.net. Retrieved December 6, 2022, from https://www.fieldforest.net/category/planting-and-harvesting-timelines

Planting Vegetables in Succession | University of Maryland Extension. (2022, August 4). Extension.umd.edu. https://extension.umd.edu/resource/planting-vegetables-succession

Poindexter, J. (2018, March 16). *19 Vegetable Garden Care & Maintenance Tips for a Successful Harvest*. MorningChores. https://morningchores.com/vegetable-garden-care/

Polomski, R. F., & Shaughnessy, D. (1999, February). *Controlling Weeds by Cultivating & Mulching*. Home & Garden Information Center | Clemson University, South Carolina. https://hgic.clemson.edu/factsheet/controlling-weeds-by-cultivating-mulching/

Quillen, A. (2016, August 23). *Cut to Size: Vegetable Garden Pruning for Beginners*. PartSelect.com. https://www.fix.com/blog/why-you-should-prune-vegetable-plants/

Quinn, M. (2016, January 5). *Growing Vine Based Crops*. Gardener's Path. https://gardenerspath.com/plants/vegetables/planting-vine-based-vegetables/

Roach, M. (2019, February 16). *10 top tips for growing root vegetables*. A Way to Garden. https://awaytogarden.com/10-top-tips-for-growing-root-vegetables/

Roades, H. (n.d.). *Plant Spacing Guide – Information On Proper Vegetable Garden Spacing*. Gardening Know How. Retrieved December 6, 2022, from https://www.gardeningknowhow.com/edible/vegetables/vgen/plant-spacing-chart.htm

Roberson, K. (2022, September 6). *8 Common Garden Pests to Look for on Your Plants and How to Get Rid of Them*. Better Homes & Gardens. https://www.bhg.com/gardening/pests/insects-diseases-weeds/garden-pest-control/

Rose, S. (2020, May 22). *Growing Mushrooms: How to Grow Specialty Mushrooms in Your Backyard*. Garden Therapy. https://gardentherapy.ca/growing-specialty-mushrooms/

Sandborn, D. (2016, September 1). *Bunny honey: Using rabbit manure as a fertilizer*. MSU Extension. https://www.canr.msu.edu/news/bunny_honey_using_rabbit_manure_as_a_fertilizer

SanSone, A. (2017, March 5). *10 Highly Effective Ways to Protect Your Garden from Critters*. Country Living. https://www.countryliving.com/gardening/garden-ideas/g4144/protect-your-garden-from-critters/

Schuh, M., Foord, K., & MacKenzie, J. (n.d.). *Growing melons in the home garden*. Extension.umn.edu. Retrieved December 6, 2022, from https://extension.umn.edu/fruit/growing-melons-home-garden

Southern States Cooperative. (2019). *How to Grow Sugar Beets* | Southern States Co-op. Southernstates.com; dotCMS dotcms.com. https://www.southernstates.com/farm-store/articles/how-to-grow-sugar-beets

Squash (Summer) Grow Guide. (n.d.). GrowVeg. Retrieved December 6, 2022, from https://www.growveg.com/plants/us-and-canada/how-to-grow-summer-squash/

Squash (Winter) Grow Guide. (n.d.). GrowVeg. Retrieved December 6, 2022, from https://www.growveg.com/plants/us-and-canada/how-to-grow-winter-squash/

Stevia Grow Guide. (n.d.). GrowVeg. Retrieved December 6, 2022, from https://www.growveg.com/plants/us-and-canada/how-to-grow-stevia/

Stevia Zone Planting Guide. (n.d.). Www.miraclegro.com. Retrieved December 6, 2022, from https://www.miraclegro.com/en-us/stevia-zone-planting-guide

Swiss Chard. (n.d.). Almanac.com. Retrieved December 6, 2022, from https://www.almanac.com/plant/swiss-chard

Tips For Growing Leafy Greens. (2022, May 6). Www.theindoorgardens.com. https://www.theindoorgardens.com/growing-leafy-greens/

Tong, C. (2021). H*arvesting and storing home garden vegetables.* Extension.umn.edu. https://extension.umn.edu/planting-and-growing-guides/harvesting-and-storing-home-garden-vegetables

Traficante. (2018, February 26). *Do Your Vegetables Have Enough Space to Grow? Soil Depth and Seed Spacing.* Mother Earth Living. https://www.motherearthliving.com/in-the-garden/grow-vegetables-soil-depth-and-seed-spacing-zb0z1802/

Treadway, A., & Crayton, E. F. (2019, May 21). *Wise Methods of Canning Vegetables.* Alabama Cooperative Extension System. https://www.aces.edu/blog/topics/food-safety/wise-methods-of-canning-vegetables/

Using Chicken Manure Safely in Home Gardens and Landscapes. (n.d.). Extension | University of Nevada, Reno. Retrieved December 6, 2022, from https://extension.unr.edu/publication.aspx?PubID=3028

Vanheems, B. (2019, February 2). *Growing Peppers from Sowing to Harves*t. GrowVeg. https://www.growveg.com/guides/growing-peppers-from-sowing-to-harvest/

When can I plant Turnips in Zone 7b. (n.d.). Frostdate.com. Retrieved December 6, 2022, from https://frostdate.com/zone/7b/turnips.htm

When to Plant Potatoes in Zone 7 and 7b: The Ultimate Guide. (2022, March 1). GFL Outdoors. https://www.gfloutdoors.com/when-to-plant-potatoes-in-zone-7-and-7b-the-ultimate-guide/

When to Plant Radishes in Zone 7 and 7b [All Factors]. (2022, March 3). GFL Outdoors. https://www.gfloutdoors.com/when-to-plant-radishes-in-zone-7-and-7b/

Where to Put a Vegetable Garden. (n.d.). Almanac.com. https://www.almanac.com/where-put-vegetable-garden

Wolken, R. (2022, March 9). *When to Plant Potatoes in Zone 7*. HappySprout. https://www.happysprout.com/inspiration/when-to-plant-potatoes-zone-7/

Made in the USA
Columbia, SC
27 September 2023

23465848R00100